STEPHEN CRANE

A Study of the Short Fiction

Also Available in Twayne's Studies in Short Fiction Series

Twayne's Studies in Short Fiction

Gordon Weaver, General Editor
Oklahoma State University

Stephen Crane.
By permission of the University of Virginia

STEPHEN CRANE

A Study of the Short Fiction

Chester L. Wolford
The Pennsylvania State University-Behrend College

TWAYNE PUBLISHERS • BOSTON
A Division of G. K. Hall & Co.

Copyright © 1989 by G. K. Hall & Co.
All rights reserved.
Published by Twayne Publishers
A Division of G. K. Hall & Co.
70 Lincoln Street, Boston, Massachusetts 02111

Copyediting supervised by Barbara Sutton.
Book design by Janet Zietowski-Reynolds.
Book production by Gabrielle B. McDonald.
Typeset in 10/12 Caslon by Compset, Inc. of Beverly, Massachusetts

Printed on permanent/durable acid-free paper
and bound in the United States of America.

Library of Congress Cataloging-in-Publication Data

Wolford, Chester L., 1944–
    Stephen Crane : a study of the short fiction / Chester L. Wolford.
      p. cm. — (Twayne's studies in short fiction ; 7)
    Bibliography: p.
    Includes index.
    ISBN 0-8057-8315-6 (alk. paper)
    1. Crane, Stephen, 1871–1900—Criticism and interpretation.
  2. Short story. I. Title. II. Series: Twayne's studies in short
fiction ; no. 7.
PS1449.C85Z984   1989
813'.4—dc19

88-35954
CIP

Contents

Preface

Stephen Crane died young: age twenty-eight years, seven months, and four days. In his last days, he was jostled by coach through England with his common-law wife, Cora Stewart; floated across the channel in a steamer; and trundled with a doctor, two nurses, a relative, and a dog, to a fashionable sanitorium in Badenweiler, Bavaria. There he died, on 5 June 1900, drowned by tuberculosis.[1]

He was born on a different continent in a different century, on 1 November 1871 in a Methodist parsonage in Newark, New Jersey, the fourteenth and last child of the Reverend Jonathan Townley Crane and Mary Helen Peck Crane. During his short, frenzied life, Crane loved a number of women: Lily Brandon Munroe, Nellie Crouse, Amy Leslie, and Cora Stewart are only those we know about. He hunted deer, bear, and partridge in rural New York. In 1895 he endured a blizzard in Nebraska and was chased by bandits across Mexico. In 1896 he was virtually run out of New York City for publicly defending a falsely arrested prostitute. In 1897 he was shipwrecked and nearly drowned off Florida, and reported on the Greco-Turkish War from Greece. In 1898 he waded into battle in Cuba and contracted the fever that hastened his death. In his last two years, he was befriended by many great writers of his time: Joseph Conrad, Henry James, H. G. Wells, Harold Frederic, and Ford Madox Ford (Hueffer), to name a few.

Crane was at home in the slums and in castles. He never chose a middle road, never the broad easy highways, but travelled always in the highlands or through the swamps. Crane may have been pleased, even amused at the end, by the many ways the distance from Newark to Badenweiler could be measured.

Those reading Stephen Crane's short fiction also face a similar problem of measurement. While Crane's characteristic use of incongruities and surprises in his fiction may divert and amuse, the uneven quality of his published works—echoing the disparate quality of his life—is often difficult to explain. Some of Crane's fiction is unparalleled and unique: "The Bride Comes to Yellow Sky," "The Blue Hotel," "The Open Boat," "The Monster," "Death and the Child," and "The Up-

Preface

turned Face." But he also produced some hurried, harried things written while he was sick unto death and in a frenzy of unsuccessful money-making to get himself out of debt by pandering to the popular taste. Crane seldom touched the heartstrings or pocketbooks of the masses when he labored at it. Nothing he ever wrote sold nearly so well as *The Red Badge of Courage*. The wonder—the great wonder—is that he wrote so much that was so good in so short a time.

The incongruities of Crane's life and work are also reflected in the variety of critical views concerning his work. So many are the angles from which Crane's fiction may be approached, in fact, that he has been seen by turns as a hack and a genius, a postmodern and an ancient, a tragedian, a comedian, a satirist, a parodist, a mythologist, a transcendentalist, an impressionist, a naturalist, an ironist, a nihilist, a writer of grand epics and slight vignettes. Critics have seen in his work the influence of Homer and Howells, Dante and Dickinson, Epicurus and Emerson, Calvin and Conrad, Tolstoy and Twain.

Crane was an extraordinarily accurate mirror of his times. Most of his fiction is concerned with five major forces that transformed American life between 1850 and 1900. First, the Civil War, only thirty years past, is reflected not only in *The Red Badge of Courage*, but also in his collection of short stories, *The Little Regiment*. Second, his many New York City sketches and Bowery tales describe accurately and often brilliantly the results of industrialization, immigration, and the accompanying growth of cities and their slums. Third, he recorded in several Western tales the passing of the American frontier. Fourth, in his Spanish-American War stories he reflected the consequences of war and Western settlement: the economic imperialism that made the Caribbean and, to some extent, the Pacific into American lakes. Finally, his impressionistic technique and nihilistic themes mirror a response—common to many intellectuals of his day—to the explosion of scientific knowledge and invention.[2] His creative reaction to the absurdity of life, although evident in his early career, did not find full expression until the very end, when he turned to ritual, those small acts that are done simply because they are done, and that carry with them a meaning that counters meaninglessness.

Even Crane's major theme has many manifestations. The predominant theme of Crane's fiction is the conflict between chaos and order, that of humanity's puny efforts to survive, to shore up fragments of order against a universe ruled by an indifferent, inexorable, and finally overwhelming chaos. Crane believed that life is chaotic; that no great purpose runs through it, none, at least, that he could find; that human destiny is dominated by chance; that, as critic Milne Holton has shown,[3] reality is almost always obscured from our vision. Even something so fundamental as hope is, to Crane, an illusion: "Hope," he said, "is a vacuous emotion."[4] Crane believed also that attempts to discover and promote any "supreme fiction," those religious, social, or political views that dominate any age or civilization—Christianity or Confucianism, capitalism or communism—derive from delusion and egotism.[5] He believed as well that the only possibility of understanding reality lies in finding and recognizing those tiny events in our lives that briefly open and shut, like a box's lid, to expose our own mistaken beliefs regarding order. The lid opens, reveals for a moment the awful truth, shuts again, and our memories go to work to alter the exposed truth. Because these moments of recognition can occur only in the minds of individuals, Crane was at best wary of groups, and at worst he loathed them.

The artistic problem Crane set for himself was to examine the ramifications of chaos, and yet find an orderly way to convey that examination. H. L. Mencken alludes to this notion when he speaks of the short story as Crane's "natural" medium. Crane's "superlative skill," Mencken says, "lay in the handling of isolated situations; he knew exactly how to depict them with a dazzling brilliance, and he knew, too, how to analyze them with penetrating insight, but beyond that he was rather at a loss: he lacked the pedestrian talent for linking one situation to another. This weakness threw him naturally into the short story, and there he was instantly at home. The short story gave him all the room he needed—and no more."[6]

If Crane lacked the talent for linking situations, it was because he did not believe situations were linked meaningfully, except in the mind. Crane's stories are, as Robert Frost says about poetry, "momentary stays against confusion." The short story became the natural form of Crane's best expressions precisely because it was ideally suited to revealing the fragmentary quality of life: the short story creates the illusion of fragmentation, in part, simply because it is so short. Because impressions are by nature brief, even fleeting, the brevity of Crane's fiction complements and makes organic his impressionistic techniques.

Shaped by image, symbol, and idea, Crane's contribution to the genre of short stories derives from this notion of the fragmentary. He was not the first to write what came to be known as "slices of life," though he was among the first, but his ability to describe and occasionally to define a "moment," "slice," or "fragment" of life helped prepare the ground for the flowering of the modern American short story during the next fifty years. Without Crane and others such as Joseph Conrad, such great writers of the next generation as William Faulkner, Katherine Anne Porter, F. Scott Fitzgerald, and Ernest Hemingway may have had to work much harder and longer to achieve the great renaissance of American fiction. For, as J. Hillis Miller says regarding Joseph Conrad—a comment equally applicable to Crane— the recognition of humanity's fragmented vision was necessary to the development of modern literature.[7]

Allied to his theme of fragmented life and fragmented vision is that of self-delusion. From the earliest stories to the last, Crane's characters try, often unconsciously, to make sense of experience, to create order out of chaos, but the order they produce is, like all forms of order, artificial. Sometimes the result is essentially comic, as in many of the early *Sullivan County Tales*, in his tales of the seaside, in a few of the late Whilomville stories, and, rather magnificently combined with tragic implications, in "The Bride Comes to Yellow Sky." Sometimes the result is high tragedy, as in "The Blue Hotel," or domestic tragedy, as in "The Monster." Often, self-delusion produces a devastating irony, as in "The Open Boat" and "Death and the Child." Only in "The Upturned Face," perhaps, does Crane find a meaningful response to chaos through ritual. Here the ritual is not that of full-blown tragedy or comedy, but the simple rituals inherent in ordinary human responses to meaninglessness.

For Crane, self-delusion derives from the enormous egotism of humanity, which he expressed many times as conceit. A famous quotation describing a particularly severe blizzard howling across Nebraska illustrates his view:

> We picture the world as thick with conquering and elate humanity, but here, with the bugles of the tempest pealing, it was hard to imagine a peopled earth. One viewed the existence of man then as a marvel, and conceded a glamour of wonder to these lice which were caused to cling to a whirling, fire-smote, ice-locked, disease-stricken, space-lost bulb. The conceit of man was explained by this storm to be the very engine of life. One was a coxcomb not to die in it.[8]

Part 1 of this volume traces the loosely chronological development of these themes in Crane's short fiction in the following order: "Tales of the Woods" (Sullivan County Tales), "Tales of the Sea and the City," "Tales of the West and Mexico," "Tales of Whilomville," and, finally, "Tales of War." Only his war stories fall outside the chronological development, for Crane's first volume of war stories, *The Little Regiment*, was published in 1896 before he had seen any war; the second volume, *Wounds in the Rain*, was published in 1900, after he had seen too much. The difference is significant.

Part 2 provides most of the very little Crane wrote about his own literary theories and practices. Unlike many writers of his day, Crane left no literary essays, no long prefaces to his works that explain his methods. Fortunately, his letters survive. Fortunate, too, that such careful and indefatigable scholars as Commander Melvin Schoberlin, Stanley Wertheim, Paul Sorrentino, and R. W. Stallman, among many others, have found so many letters that easily might have been lost. The fruit of their labors appears in *The Correspondence of Stephen Crane*, edited by Stanley Wertheim and Paul Sorrentino. This is perhaps the first critical book on Crane to have the advantage of that text.

Part 3 reprints critical appraisals. Many critics have written about different sides of Crane's work. My first criterion for selection was quality; the second was range. Although several critics have written well about Crane's impressionism, for example, few have written convincingly about the influence of specific writers. If nothing else, Crane's sources are elusive.

All in-text citations of Crane's stories refer to the University of Virginia edition of his complete works (10 vols., 1969–76).

Notes

1. R. W. Stallman, *Stephen Crane: A Biography* (New York: George Braziller, 1968), 515.

2. Lars Åhnebrink, *The Beginnings of Naturalism in American Fiction: A Study of the Works of Hamlin Garland, Stephen Crane, and Frank Norris with Special Reference to Some European Influences: 1891–1903*, vol. 9 of *Essays and Studies in American Language and Literature*, ed. S. B. Liljegran (New York: Russell & Russell, 1950), 1.

3. Milne Holton, *Cylinder of Vision: The Fiction and Journalistic Writing of Stephen Crane* (Baton Rouge: Louisiana State University Press, 1972).

4. John Berryman, *Stephen Crane* (Cleveland: World Publishing Company, 1950), 252.

5. Coined by Wallace Stevens (1879–1955), the term "Supreme Fic-

tion" means any set of beliefs that give order and meaning to humanity and the universe and which are held by great numbers of people. Any of the great religious and political movements of history qualifies as a Supreme Fiction: Christianity, Marxism, Buddhism, Islam, and the like.

Stevens attended Crane's funeral at the Metropolitan Temple in New York (See Stallman, *Stephen Crane*, 520.).

6. H. L. Mencken, "Introduction," *The Work of Stephen Crane*, vol. 10, ed. Wilson Follett (New York: Alfred A. Knopf, Inc., 1926), ix–xiii. Reprinted in *Stephen Crane's Career: Perspectives and Evaluations*, ed. Thomas A. Gullason (New York: New York University Press, 1972), 94–96.

7. J. Hillis Miller, *Poets of Reality* (Cambridge, Mass.: Harvard University Press, 1965), 3ff.

8. "The Blue Hotel," in *University of Virginia Edition of the Works of Stephen Crane* (Charlottesville: University Press of Virginia, 1969–76), 5:165.

Acknowledgments

I gratefully acknowledge the following.

Paul Sorrentino, Stanley Wertheim, and the Columbia University Press for permission, generously and kindly given, to use the galleys of, and a number of letters from, their splendid and indispensable *The Correspondence of Stephen Crane*.

Richard Winslow III, librarian and researcher's researcher; Victor Susol, research assistant; and Norma Hartner.

Harrison Meserole, Milne Holton, Keith Fort, Willis Regier, and Dean Baldwin for their dedication to the profession of letters.

John Lilley, Provost and Dean of The Pennsylvania State University-Behrend College, and John Magenau, Director of The School of Business, for their generous support for this project.

The University Press of Virginia for permission to quote from *The Works of Stephen Crane*, the ten-volume standard text, edited by Fredson Bowers.

Reeve and Rebecca, truly the best and the brightest.

Part 1

THE SHORT FICTION:
A CRITICAL ANALYSIS

Tales of the Woods
and Other Early Stories

In 1883, when Crane was about eleven, his older brother, William Howe Crane, began to practice law in Port Jervis, New York. About the same time he helped found the Hartwood Club, a semi-exclusive hunting and fishing camp in nearby Sullivan County. Over the years, Stephen stayed often at the camp, hunting and, presumably, fishing. He also did a little writing there. In mid-June of 1891, when he was nineteen, Crane and three friends—Frederic M. Lawrence, Louis E. Carr, Jr., and Louis C. Senger, Jr.—spent some time camping there. This trip and these experiences produced those stories that have become known as *The Sullivan County Tales and Sketches*, the first fiction for which he was paid.

Crane began writing long before 1891. It is fortunate that much of this early work has been retrieved, for it shows in simpler outlines the themes and methods that later would become more sophisticated. Crane's earliest story, "Uncle Jake and the Bell Handle" (8:3–7), may have been written as early as 1885, when Crane was thirteen or fourteen.[1] In this story, two country bumpkins—a farmer and his niece—travel in a horse-drawn wagon from the farm to the city to sell Jake's produce. The description of their entrance into the city emphasizes chaos: "Soon the houses began to appear closer together, there were more tin cans and other relics strewn about the road-side, they began to get views of multitudes of back-yards, with washes on lines; grimy, smoky factories; stock yards filled with discordant mobs of beasts; whole trains of freight cars, standing on tracks; dirty children, homeless dogs and wandering pigs. To Uncle Jake's experienced eye, this denoted that they were entering the city"(8:4). Chaos is recreated here by the sheer number of details crowded into very few words. Tin cans, washing, factories, freight cars, children, dogs, and pigs, all crowd together indiscriminately. Crane's attempt to organize his fiction by surrounding the pandemonium with houses fails.

The insistence on *seeing,* so prominent in all Crane's fiction, is pres-

3

ent in the houses that "began to appear," and in the back-yards of which Jake and his niece "began to get views." The delusions that result from fear, egotism, and fragmentary knowledge are also apparent here through Uncle Jake's behavior when he moves into territories with which he is unfamiliar. Arriving in town, Uncle Jake sells his produce, buys supplies, and finally, to show his niece the wonders of the city, takes her to a hotel, where he indulges his curiosity in the hotel parlor:

> He wandered about the room, running his hands over the picture frames and feeling of the upholstery of the chairs.
>
> In an evil hour, he came upon the bell-handle.
>
> . . . . He looked at it for some time. . . . Finally he pulled it.
>
> Now it came to pass, that, at precisely that moment, a waiter of the hotel made a terrific onslaught on a gong that was sure to make any horses in the vicinity run away and awaken all the late sleepers for blocks around. (8:5)

Thinking that he has caused the uproar, Uncle Jake subsequently believes that he has become "a fergitive from justice, a critir hounded by the dogs of the law!" He takes what comfort he can from the situation: "Thank goodness, Saree," he tells his niece, "that the militia can't be called out on such short notice and they'll have time to find out that it is a mistake. To see this country plunged into er civil war by the hand of an ignorant old man, would be terr'ble" (8:6).

Juvenile humor this may be, but Crane's themes of chaos versus order, of egotism and self-delusion, and of limited vision in a world of chance are already apparent. Uncle Jake is an ignorant man, but not for the reason he believes. He believes that he was ignorant of the bell-ringing's criminality. Actually, he is ignorant of two things: that he did not cause the noise and that no one cares whether he did or not. Even the narrator's ironic commentary, so characteristic of Crane's later fiction, adds a sophistication rarely found in the words of teenagers: most things in the story are seen through "Uncle Jake's experienced eye." In this story chaos is caused not only "out there" in the universe, but also within Uncle Jake himself, as a result of his misperception of the way things are.

About the time he was twenty, Crane began writing stories about the wilderness, usually set in the woods in Sullivan County, New York, and Pike County, Pennsylvania, where he spent part of 1892 hunting, fishing, and writing in and around his brother's camp. Crane himself regarded them as "articles of many kinds," part fiction, part journalism.[2] And, indeed, his is a fair estimate, for while many of the "sketches"[3] are not up to Crane's later standards, others remain fine examples of his early fiction. They are also significant as Crane's first sustained and serious attempts to display his imagination in stories having a common setting and theme.

The vast wilderness that once was the New World has always fascinated Americans; even, or perhaps especially, when it existed only in our minds, as, for the most part, it did by the 1890s. Among the literary traditions spawned by the wilderness is the tall tale and one of its progeny, the hunting yarn. Crane seems to have been extraordinarily well-versed in this tradition.[4] In one sketch, entitled "The Way in Sullivan County: A Study in the Evolution of the Hunting Yarn" (8:220–22), Crane demonstrates considerable knowledge:

> A country famous for its hunting and its hunters is naturally prolific of liars. . . . Every man cultivates what taste he has for prevarication lest his neighbors look down on him. One can buy sawlogs from a native and take his word that the bargain is square, but ask the same man how many deer he has killed in his lifetime and he will stop working . . . and paralyze the questioner with a figure that would look better than most of the totals to the subscription list for monuments to national heroes. The inhabitants [are wise to one another]. . . . The only real enjoyment is when the unoffending city man appears. . . . In a shooting country, no man should tell just exactly what he did. He should tell what he would have liked to do or what he expected to do, just as if he accomplished it. (8:220–21)

The hunting yarn normally depends for its humor on making the improbable, sometimes even the impossible, seem probable. These sketches, then, are humorous tales, filled with the high spirits of youth and country folk. In Crane's day, and in some areas even today, young men commonly went to the woods, not like Thoreau, "to transact some business," but rather to have fun, unencumbered by the demands of polite society or even the day-to-day rules of behavior required of people in towns and cities.

In these stories, people *impose* order where there is only chaos and its main effect: chance. In several of *The Sullivan County Tales*, for example, the perception of order and the reality of chaos is the only real theme. One of the most common impositions of order where there is none is that of attributing intelligence and purpose to nature. The humor derives from the same theme that will later take on tragic and ironic proportions in Crane's work: the difference between perception and reality.

The main character of these tales is "the little man." Prefiguring many of Crane's great characters, "the little man" is vain, naive, terribly concerned with what people think of him, curious, and possessed of about the same degrees of foolhardiness and cowardice as are most of us. Moreover, like the great characters, "the little man" is isolated from his environment.

One good illustration is provided by "The Mesmeric Mountain" (8:269–71).[5] In this story a "little man" gets lost in the woods. After walking miles, he is not only lost, but also tired. Taking his bearings from a nearby mountain, he tries to move away from the mountain only to find himself several times still at its foot. In near panic, he endows the mountain with intelligence and mobility: " 'it's been follerin' me!' he grovelled" (8:271). In his fear, he becomes angry and, to the reader, foolish: "As he felt the heel of the mountain about to crush his head, he sprang again to his feet. . . . The little man then made an attack. He climbed . . ." (8:271). After a long and frenzied climb, the little man reaches the top. Having conquered the mountain, the little man surveys his world with great pride, but the reader is reminded of the truth in the last sentence: "The mountain under his feet was motionless" (8:271). *Still* motionless.

Another of Crane's early *Sullivan County Tales*. "The Octopush" (8:230–33), illustrates Crane's method of conveying impressions in the mind of the characters, impressions the reader recognizes as ridiculous. It illustrates as well Crane's method of pointing to the difference between reality and illusion, chaos and order. In "The Octopush," four men go fishing in a big, shallow pond made by damming a stream after the trees of the surrounding forest have been cut down. The stumps from many of these trees stick out of the water. The adventurers hire a local man with a boat to carry them each to one of these stumps. The boatman then leaves, promising to return before dark, but he does not return. Each man is left on a stump to contemplate his predicament. The reader sees the situation as humorous in the tradition of the old "city-slicker goes to the woods" tradition. The humor is heightened by the absurdity of the fishermen's impressions:

> A ghost-like mist came and hung upon the waters. The pond became a grave-yard. The grey tree-trunks dank dark logs turned to

monuments and crypts. Fire-flies were wisp-lights dancing over graves, and then, taking regular shapes, appeared like brass nails in crude caskets. The individual began to gibber. . . . The little man began to sob; another groaned and the two remaining, being timid by nature, swore great lurid oaths which blazed against the sky. (8:233)

The boatman, drunk, returns late at night, announcing himself with a drunken, ridiculous howl, but the voice in the dark "raised the hair on the four men's heads. . . ."

As if taking his cue from Ecclesiastes, Crane wrote many of these stories to expose the truth of the Preacher's cry: "Vanity of vanities. All is vanity." Just as the hunter must lie to preserve his image as a hunter, so must others accept "dares" and otherwise do things to preserve their own standing in a male world of "honor." In "The Holler Tree" (8:259–264), for example, a series of turnabouts occur, all dealing with vanity. The story begins as the same four men are returning to camp after securing provisions. While the little man and the pudgy man are arguing over the degree of care to be taken carrying eggs, they spy a huge, dead hollow tree, broken off at the top. The little man suggests that the tree contains many things inside, and the pudgy man suggests that the little man climb the tree to find out. Not wanting to appear afraid, the little man climbs the tree. When he arrives at the top, he can see nothing: "It's dark." The little man falls inside the trunk. Trapped there, the little man becomes angry and shakes the tree. It nearly falls on the pudgy man who, brave until now, runs madly away and leaps, just out of the tree's reach. The others pull the little man from the base of the tree. He sees the pudgy man and becomes proud of his own behavior, seeing it as superior to that of the pudgy man. As the little man walks away, "his stride was that of a proud grenadier" (8:264).

Most of the sketches are told with the same irony, the same contrast between expectation and performance, between illusion and reality, that characterizes all of Crane's fiction. Two sketches in particular demonstrate the cynical, almost nihilistic side of Crane's work. These are early stories, however, and they tend to preach a bit. And, as Crane said later, "preaching is fatal to art."[6]

Perhaps the most bitterly ironical, illusion-deflating, and least fictional is "The Last of the Mohicans" (8:199–201).[7] In this sketch, Crane provides an outline for the same method he was to use later: he exposes and repudiates illusion and what he considers to be bad art, that which perpetuates illusion. In particular, he rails against the same writer that Twain excoriated in "Fenimore Cooper's Literary Offenses." Sullivan County natives, Crane writes, "are continually shaking metaphorical fists at 'The Last of the Mohicans' of J. Fenimore Cooper. . . . No consideration for the author, the literature or the readers can stay their hands, and they claim without reservation that the last of the Mohicans . . . was a demoralized dilapidated inhabitant of Sullivan County" (8:199). Crane parodies both Cooper's heroic Indian character, Uncas, and Cooper's prose style: "All know well . . . that bronze god in a North American wilderness, that warrior with the eye of the eagle, the ear of the fox, the tread of a catlike panther, and the tongue of the wise serpent of fable" (8:200). Crane's, and Sullivan County's, last Mohican "was no warrior who yearned after the blood of his enemies as the hart panteth for the water-brooks; on the contrary he developed a craving for the rum of the white man which rose superior to all other anxieties. . . . He dragged through his life in helpless misery" (8:200–201). In this sketch, as Crane says, "the pathos lies in the contrast between the noble savage of fiction and the sworn-to claimant of Sullivan County" (8:200).

The tables are turned in another sketch about Indians and white men called "Not Much of A Hero" (8:211–15). In this sketch the famous Indian fighter, Tom Quick, is examined as legend and fact. The natives of Sullivan County are no longer the staunch purveyors of truth that they are in "The Last of the Mohicans." This time they have erected over a grave a monument inscribed "Tom Quick, the Indian Slayer, or the Avenger of the Delaware." A "cheap edition of Tom Quick's alleged biography" pictures him as "a gory-handed avenger of an advanced type who goes about seeking how many Indians he can devour within a given time. He is a paragon of virtue and slaughters savages in a very high and exalted manner" (8:212). A more accurate historic account, however, cites Quick as a crazed man who kills innocent Indians in their sleep; he exhibits no virtue, no skill, no morality. For the first time, Crane ends a sketch with the ambiguity that later reaches perfection in "The Open Boat": Quick may have been "one of the sturdy bronzed woodsmen who cleared the path of civilization," or he may have been simply "a monomaniac upon the subject of Indians," or he may have been "a man whose hands were stained with unoffending blood, purely and simply a murderer" (8:215).

These two sketches, although slight, provide clear examples of the methods Crane employed throughout his career. Several of the better sketches, all written only weeks or months later, demonstrate how quickly Crane's skills improved.[8] The contrast between illusion and reality provides the major method for several of these sketches, as well as the source for their humorous effects.

"Four Men in A Cave" (8:225–30) was published only two months after "Not Much of A Hero," but unlike the other story, this one is completely fictional. Four men, including the little man, are camping, and they agree to explore a nearby cave, saying "We can tell a great tale when we get back to the city" (8:225). After lighting knotted roots of pitch pine, they crawl through the cave until they slip and fall down a steep incline to the bottom. Once there, they find a dry, level place with a bed, a table, and a man who frightens the little man into playing cards with him, during which he takes all the little man's money. When the little man loses all his money, the "recluse" chases them from the cave. Returning to camp, they discover from their guide that the man is Tom Gardner, who went mad after losing everything he had—family included—in a card game. The little man curses, and the others mock him by quoting his own words to him: "We can tell a great tale when we get back to the city."

The humor of the story is conveyed by exposing vanity and contrasting it to fear. The little man had suggested the exploration out of curiosity and bravado. When they determine which of the four should go first into the cave—there is room only for one at a time—"they fought for last place and the little man was overcome" (8:225–26). Frightened, the little man says several times, "Ho. Let's go back." The others refuse: "The others were not brave. They were last." The contrast between the bravado of the beginning, the cowardice of the middle, and the anger of the end also contributes to the humor. This humor depends almost entirely on the difference between expectation and reality. Even the description of Tom Gardner—his ghoulish appearance in a formalized, almost ritualized setting, is rather unsettling—is not sufficient to suppress the reader's realization that there is only one of him and four of them.

Although the little man is part of a group, the reader gets little sense of solidarity among them. Indeed, the others say nothing as Gardner takes all the little man's money. And not even the most ardent spelunker will suggest that dark, damp, dangerous caves are natural environments for city folk. The little man is finally isolated from his companions, from his environment, and from the reality of a poor, addled hermit who appears to be only what each of the four men calls him: "vampire," "ghoul," "Druid before the sacrifice," and "the shade of an Aztec witch doctor" (8:228).

The clearest instance of deflating expectations in these stories appears in a weird tale called "A Ghoul's Accountant." In this story, however, the deflation does not occur in the little man. He is so befuddled and short of time to collect his thoughts that he cannot have expectations open to deflation. The deflation is literary, and occurs in the reader.

The story opens in camp before daylight. The fire is nearly out, and all four campers are asleep. All things, in short, are as they should be. Then comes the following description, worthy of the script from a second-rate horror film.

> Off in the gloomy unknown a foot fell upon a twig. The laurel leaves shivered at the stealthy passing of danger. A moment later a man [with "fiercely red" skin and "whiskers infinitely black"] crept into the spot of dim light [from the embers of the fire]. He gazed at the four passive bundles and smiled a smile that curled his lips and showed yellow, disordered teeth. The campfire . . . expired. The voices of the trees grew hoarse and frightened. The bundles were stolid. (8:240)

Using a "three-pronged pickerel-spear," "the ghoul" wakens the little man, and, while the other three men continue sleeping, forces the little man off and into the black forest. At this point the reader may be excited: things do not bode well for the little man. When the ghoul and the little man arrive at a house, the windows of which are "yellow-papered," they discover "a wild, gray man." But deflation occurs with the first words of the gray man: " 'Stranger,' he said suddenly, 'how much is thirty-three bushels of pertater at sixty-four an' a half a bushel?' " (8:242). Somehow the little man manages to give the correct answer, the ghoul and the gray man argue, and then the latter kicks the little man out the door. The surprise ending, although intentional, serves only to deflate the expectations of the reader as well as of the protagonist. The reader is less surprised than disappointed. Crane has not yet gained complete control over his talents.

"The Cry of the Huckleberry Pudding" has the same motif as "A Ghoul's Accountant," but this time the reader is let in on the joke early. The little man makes a bad huckleberry pudding, nearly all of which the little man is compelled to eat when the other three refuse more than a bite. Later that night the three are wakened by terrible noises in the woods. There follow long descriptions of the horror in the woods which frightens them: "Their faces twitched and their fingers turned to wax. The cry was repeated. Its burden caused the men to huddle together like drowning kittens. They watched the banshees. . . . They heard a thousand approaching footfalls. . . . They grovelled" (8:256). Then the narrator indulges in hyperbole—trying to get as much from the joke as he can—by describing the noise as from some monster powerful enough to shake the ground: "they heard the unknown . . . giving calls, weighted with challenge, that could make cities hearing, fear. Roars went to the ends of the earth and, snarls that would appall armies . . ." (8:256). After having "reached the cellar of fear" and having noticed that there were only three of them ("It's got Billie" [8:257]), the three men cautiously look for the source of the horror. They find the little man howling in agony from a stomachache caused by the bad pudding. Embarrassed at having been frightened, the three men upbraid the little man. The little man can do little but chide them for applying "no salve but moral teaching to a man with a stomachache" (8:259).

A silly tale, but its motif remains important in Crane. Throughout Crane's fiction, characters become frightened by the unknown only to discover their fears to be unwarranted, or they assume the unknown to be known and have no fear, only to discover too late, or almost too late, that the unknown was indeed to be feared.

Only once in these tales does Crane manage to transcend the naturalistic view of the mind as purely mechanistic. In "Killing His Bear" (8:249–51), there occurs a complete, although temporary, disorientation. The story is also one of the most graphic, even chilling, descriptions in American literature of a hunter killing an animal. Only Faulkner surpasses it.

A hunter, presumably standing on a game trail, hears a hound yelping in the distance. When the bear emerges from some thickets, Crane elicits sympathy by describing the bear as running "like a frightened kitten" (8:250). The bear is concerned only with the hound behind him and does not know of the "thing with death standing motionless in the shadows before him" (8:251). The hunter draws a bead on the bear, "searching swiftly over the dark shape. Under the fore-shoulder was the place. A chance to pierce the heart, sever an artery or pass through the lungs" (8:251). Immediately before he fires, "the earth faded to nothing. Only space and the game, the aim and the hunter. Mad emotions, powerful enough to rock worlds, hurled through the little man . . ." (8:251). When he fired, "creation rocked and the bear stumbled." This is the first imperfect instance in Crane's fiction of the moment of recognition, the instant of reality in which the wide world becomes microcosmic, and there remain "only space and the game." It is also the first instance of the expression of that reality's fleeting nature, for the hunter loses the preciousness of the moment, the sacredness, and he diminishes himself by his reaction:

> "Hit!" he yelled, and ran on. Some hundred yards forward he came to a dead bear with his nose in the snow. . . . A mad froth lay in the animal's open mouth and his limbs were twisted in agony.
> The little man yelled again and sprang forward, waving his hat as if he were leading the cheering of thousands. He ran up and kicked the ribs of the bear. Upon his face was the smile of a successful lover. (8:251)

Most of *The Sullivan County Tales* are humorous and display the apprenticeship of a fine writer. Occasionally, however, as in "Killing His Bear," we are given a glimpse of the apprenticeship of a genius.

Tales of the Sea and the City

After spending the summer of 1891 in the Sullivan County woods, Crane moved to New York City, where he spent the winter observing the slums of the Bowery and the Tenderloin, observations that produced not only *Maggie*, but many "Bowery" and "Tenderloin" stories and sketches as well. And the summer in Asbury Park that followed the summer in Sullivan County produced a number of Asbury Park sketches and a few stories.

Among those stories of the seaside is "The Pace of Youth" (5:3–12). Although much of Crane's fiction combines "deflationary realism" with "the dazzle of appearances,"[9] "The Pace of Youth" fairly sings the tune of youth: it reads like a race in the sunshine with speed, airiness, love in bloom, and a sense of youth's inevitable victory in its battle against age. Age is the girl's father, Stimson, who is played in slow, ponderous chords, heavy, dark, brooding, and, because the story is a romantic comedy, foolish.

A description of "Stimson's Mammoth Merry-Go-Round" and of the area surrounding it opens the story. There is the "soft boom of the surf"; "cries of bathers"; flags; ships with painted sails; and a great hawk drifting slowly in "the still, sunshot air" (5:3). The merry-go-round glitters in "a never-ending race" of "tireless racers" on the wooden ponies and giraffes "that made Stimson's machine magnificent and famous" (5:4). Stimson himself is less attractive. He is a fierce, glowering man with "indomitable whiskers" (5:3). He is also angry that the young man he has hired to run the merry-go-round is "makin' eyes at 'Lizzie," Stimson's daughter. Amazed that "any youth should dare smile at the daughter in the presence of the august father" (5:4), Stimson watches the budding romance between the youth and 'Lizzie, who is the ticket-taker for the merry-go-round.

'Lizzie and the youth continue to look at each other for some time, until finally, "they knew that to live without each other would be a wandering in deserts" (5:6): At this point, the blocking figure, Stimson, "a resolute man" who "never hesitated to grapple with a problem," decides to "overturn everything at once" (5:7). He forbids 'Lizzie her "everlasting grinning at that idiot" (5:7) and threatens to

13

fire the youth unless he stops looking at 'Lizzie. Both seem to be cowed by the old man, and Stimson stands "in fine satisfaction": "Through his mind went the proud reflection that people who came in contact with his granite will usually ended in quick and abject submission" (5:7). But the pace of youth is such that the young boy and girl soon find means to take walks on the beach together in the evenings without her father's knowledge. Sometime later, Stimson is astounded to find that they are running away together: "Stimson gave vent to a dreadful roar" (5:10). He hires a horse-drawn hack and speeds away in pursuit of the fleeing couple. Standing in the back seat, Stimson spurs the driver to hurry, and soon believes he is gaining on them.

The story ends with a description of the race: "Ahead the other carriage had been flying with speed, as from realization of the menace in the rear. It bowled away rapidly, drawn by the eager spirit of a young and modern horse. . . . [Stimson] began to feel impotent; his whole expedition was the tottering of an old man upon the trail of birds. A sense of age made him choke with wrath. That other vehicle, that was youth, with youth's pace, it was swift flying with the hope of dreams. He began to comprehend . . . the power of their young blood, the power to fly strongly into the future and feel and hope again, even at a time when his bones must be laid in the earth" (5:12).

Even in this early story, Crane knows intuitively what he is after. The omniscient narrator describes Stimson in the moment of his recognition that the pace of youth is too fast for him: "Stimson sat back with the astonishment and grief of a man who has been defied by the universe" (5:12). And the last line presents an early example of Crane's ambiguous endings: "At last he made a gesture. It meant that at any rate he was not responsible" (5:12). On the one hand, he *is* responsible. By refusing to allow the young couple to court, he drives them into each other's arms. On the other hand, he *is not* responsible, for the pace of youth is forever faster than that of age, forever demanding, and getting, its moment in the sun.

In another story, the action moves from the seaside to the sea itself. Here, a bathhouse attendant, charged with renting bathing suits, gives the wrong size suit to one of the two protagonists, called throughout the story the "freckled man." The freckled man says, "it ain't a bathing-suit. . . . It's an auditorium. . . ." (8:16), thus precipitating the long chain of humorous misperceptions Crane titles "The Reluctant Voyagers" (8:14–33).

The attendant may have provided a suit too big because he "was looking at the world with superior eyes through a hole in a board"

(8:15). Almost never listed with Crane's better stories, "The Reluctant Voyagers" should be, for it is a well-designed piece that provides glimpses of Crane's impressionistic methods. The story has a limited third-person persona, which, as Nagel says, is "the natural expression of Literary Impressionism."[10] Furthermore, examples of limited vision are everywhere in the story, not only in the attendant's "hole in a board." The egotism as the "engine of life" appears here, as well as the great fear of the unknown and the subsequent tricks of the mind. At one point, for example, Crane renders a literal perception uninterpreted by normal understanding: "Three ships fell off the horizon" (8:19). This is the mind using not what it has been told to see, but what it actually sees.

After finding a raft, falling asleep, and drifting at sea, the two men wake and argue. The tall man blames the freckled man for being so vain about the ill-fitting suit that they had to swim away from others out to a raft. There is real fear hidden in humorous whining: "you have murdered your best friend" (8:19).

Because the seascapes are elemental and reduce perspectives to a few geometrical shapes, the scene—two men sitting on a raft on the ocean—provides a simple setting for a young writer beginning to work with literary impressionism. The sunset is not called a sunset but rather "fires in the west" (8:20); reflections on the water of lights on shore are described this way: "red and green lights began to dot the blackness" (8:20).

Losing their frames of normal reference as the sky becomes as black as the water, the two men become frightened. And to their limited vision is joined downright misperception. Robbed of most of their sight, the tall man indulges in wishes and the freckled man begins to imagine things:

> "I see things comin'," murmured the freckled man.
> "I wish I hadn't ordered that new dress suit for the hop [dance] tomorrow night," said the tall man reflectively. . . .
> "Somebody's here," whispered the freckled man.
> "I wish I had an almanac," remarked the tall man, regarding the moon.
> (8:20)

Both misunderstand their situation. The tall man underplays its seriousness. They could, after all, die. The freckled man, on the other hand, begins to imagine a kind of malevolent force in the darkness.

Such imaginings occur in real life, although few people have experienced them. They are, one supposes, related to the common primitive and childish fear of things that go bump in the night. Many people lost and alone on the sea for a long time have remarked, when rescued, that they could not get over the feeling that some unseen person was with them on their craft. Crane may have heard such a story and incorporated it here.

Finally, the freckled man resorts to calling on a higher being: "Providence will not leave us" (8:21). The tall man, more cynical, is nevertheless able to aim hope in a different direction: "Oh, we'll be picked up soon. I owe money" (8:21).

Cold and lonely, the two men shiver in the dark until a ship comes by. The tall man expects a glorious rescue from "kind sailors in blue and white" who will take them aboard, "where the handsome, bearded captain . . . will welcome us" (8:21). Once on board, however, the reluctant voyagers, shivering in their wet swimming suits, find themselves the objects of laughter. "The tall man grew furious. . . . 'This rescue ain't right'" (8:23). Later, the tall man attacks the captain, grabbing him by the throat: "If you laugh again, I'll kill you" (8:27). The tall man cannot believe that the Captain will not turn his ship around, return to the New Jersey resort town, and put them ashore. The ship arrives in New York City, and the captain plans to drop the two men there. All in all, a rather reasonable arrangement. Finally set ashore at New York City by a justifiably furious ship's captain, the two men hail a cab and head off for Park Place, the most fashionable and expensive address in the city.

The story is a study in egotism and self-delusion. The two men became stranded out of vanity: the freckled man was ashamed to be seen in a ridiculously over-sized bathing suit. At the story's end, it is the tall man's vanity that makes him attack the captain and in general display himself as a fool. Appearing at the New York City docks in less than appropriate attire is humiliating. Never mind that they had beat great odds in being picked up at all, and that their lives had been saved.

The very end of the story, as with many of Crane's endings, provides yet another reversal in assigning responsibility for the reluctant voyage. The freckled man upbraids the tall man: "I think the time is ripe to point out to you that your obstinacy, your selfishness, your villainous temper and your various other faults can make it just as unpleasant for your own self, my dear boy, as they frequently do for other people" (8:33). This from the man whose "faults" got them in trouble in the first place. And speaking from a mountain of superiority to which he has little right, the freckled man concludes the story: "I most sincerely hope . . . that I shall soon see signs in you which shall lead me to believe that you have become a wiser man" (8:33). Neither man is wiser, for neither has learned anything from his experiences. Self-delusion, an important variation on Crane's primary theme of chaos and order, provides a humorous story here. In other stories, however, the theme produces more serious implications.

Like "The Reluctant Voyagers," the most famous of Crane's "sea tales" is set on the sea, and has to do with ego, pride, and survival. The difference is that "The Open Boat" (5:68–92) also has to do with death. Further, it displays the difference between Crane's skills in 1892, when he wrote a story he had only imagined, and 1897, when he wrote a story the events of which he had lived. On 1 January 1897, Crane was on a rusty old freighter, the *Commodore*, ultimately bound, it is often supposed, for Cuba. It may have been carrying arms for the Cuban insurgents. On 2 January, her seams opened after having rammed a sandbar on New Year's Day, the *Commodore* sank, and on 3 January, Crane was still on the sea with three others in a ten-foot dinghy, rowing for his life. One of the men, an oiler named William Higgins, died on the way in, struck on the head by timbers tossing in the surf. Crane, exhausted and dazed but alive, had been lucky.

"The Open Boat" strikes the familiar themes of confrontation with death, and of one's insignificance in an indifferent universe, but the narrative perspective is more personal, for the protagonist experiences the same close brush with death that Crane himself had experienced. Despite nearly drowning, Crane maintains an ironic stance in "The Open Boat," and in this story the irony is especially natural, unobtrusive, and effective, deeply embedded in the texture of the prose. John Berryman, a poet and biographer of Crane, once referred to the ubiquitous irony in Crane's fiction as a manifestation of his "irony of soul." Irony seems to have been so much a part of Crane the man that its appearance in all his fiction is almost entirely unaffected.

"The Open Boat" is, as Conrad said, "a symbolic tale." It recounts an archetypal journey of discovery during which four men are tested to their limits. Moreover, these four compose a microcosm of society or of humanity. There is the formal head, who also proves to be a natural leader: Captain Murphy. At bottom is the follower, the cook—a somewhat corpulent, dependent, and incompetent man who must be prodded into working for his and the others' survival. In between there is the "good" man, the oiler Billy Higgins (of whose "splendid manhood" Crane wrote in the newspaper account),[11] and the correspondent, the "eyes" of the story.

The story opens with a line now famous: "None of them knew the color of the sky." In fact, all sense of certainty is gone. Once again, as in the caves and the woods, the protagonist finds himself outside his normal environment. Although they know the color of the sea, uncertainty is increased by the lack of frames of reference: "Their eyes glanced level, and were fastened on the waves that swept toward them. These waves were of the hue of slate, save for the tops, which were of foaming white, and all of the men knew the color of the sea. The horizon narrowed and widened, and dipped and rose . . ." (5:68). Completely absorbed in the job of staying afloat, the four men have no leisure to think about the sky, to think, in other words, about the meaning or significance of their lives. They talk briefly about their chances of making it ashore. Sometimes they are hopeful, sometimes not.

A few people on shore notice them but believe them to be fishing. Exhausted, hungry, and cold, they spend another night on the ocean, all but the wounded captain taking turns at the oars. Next morning, the captain decides that, as they are too tired to try to stay afloat all day, they must go in through the surf. They do; the boat capsizes as they had feared; but three of the four make it safely to shore. The oiler, who had seemed the strongest, drowns.

"The Open Boat" is overtly symbolic, and hence so open to interpretation that it is perhaps the most often interpreted story in the Crane canon. So many interpretations have been advanced, in fact, that it would be impossible even to mention most of them here. But the ambiguity that leads to so many interpretations perhaps *is* itself the interpretation. The story seems to lead to the existential proposition that no one can know anything.[12] Not only is the color of the sky unknown, and the horizon always shifting, but the men interpret and misinterpret things constantly. Now the "rescue station" must be here, then there; now the life-saving station is further north or it is not; now the station is manned or it is not. People on shore see them and they are saved, then they do not and they are not. The lights they see at night come from this town or that town. A monolithic tower stands on shore, indifferent, putting the lie to all notions of a benevolent and caring Providence: "The tower . . . was a giant, standing with its back to the plight of ants" (5:88). They know nothing.

These constant shiftings of seeming to know and then not knowing are symbolic of all knowledge. Ultimately, all that matters is the individual consciousness. The correspondent begins to express himself ritualistically: "If I am going to be drowned—if I am going to be drowned—if I am going to be drowned, why, in the name of the seven mad gods who rule the sea, why was I allowed to come thus far and contemplate sand and trees?" (5:84).

Then he advances to a new thought: "When it occurs to a man that nature does not regard him as important, and that she feels she would not maim the universe by disposing of him, he at first wishes to throw bricks at the temple, and he hates deeply the fact that there are no bricks and temples" (5:84–85). The "subtle brotherhood" born of necessity in the boat falls apart as they dump individually into the sea and one of them dies. On shore, trapped inside their own thoughts, each is alone.

Presumably fed, clothed, and rested, the three survivors and their feelings are described by the narrator: "When it came night, the white waves paced to and fro in the moonlight, and the wind brought the sound of the great sea's voice to the men on shore, and they felt that they could then be interpreters" (5:92) of what it is like to be near death, what it is like to have believed they were going to die, of the great sea's voice as one of indifference. But that is all.

Crane is always ironical. In fact, the more plaintive the ending, and the more lyrical, the more ironic.[13] On one level the irony is simply that the "voice" is indifferent. On another level, the level of Crane's attempts to face death—seen in a dozen stories—the irony provides no resolution. The ritualistic responses of the correspondent point to an incomplete resolution that does not become complete until the later story, "The Upturned Face." In "The Open Boat," the protagonist does not know the truth evident in ritual, perhaps because he has not died. Possibly, for a moment on the water, he knew something. But, as always with Crane, apprehension of reality is at best fleeting. This story and this interpretation are, as the story's subtitle suggests, tales "intended to be told after the fact."

Before coming to the symbolic but almost matter-of-fact expression of a nihilistic naturalism in "The Open Boat," Crane leaned toward some of the more obvious beliefs of naturalism; these are most clearly set forth in his city tales of the Bowery. On the cover of a copy of *Maggie, A Girl of the Streets,* Crane wrote that the book tries to show that "environment is a tremendous thing."[14] Many of his early short stories about city life similarly display the trappings of the socially committed naturalist: slums, immigrants, harmful drugs, alcohol, violence, and an overwhelming sense of entrapment.

The Bowery sketches are interesting for giving a picture of life in that place at that time. These sketches, written primarily for the newspapers, include "An Eloquence of Grief " (8:382–84), and several pieces about the "Tenderloin" district of the city, the most infamous section of an infamous neighborhood.[15] "Yen-Hock Bill and His Sweetheart" (8:396–99), a story about the egotism and cruelty of such people, is only one of "three fully fictional Tenderloin stories."[16] "Opium's Varied Dreams" (8:365–70) may be taken as typical.

In "Opium's Varied Dreams," Crane presents a cold, unemotional, and reportorial picture of "opium fiends." He begins by laying aside the common notion of the time that the Chinese were alone in their abuse of opium by saying that of the 25,000 opium smokers in New York City, most were "white men and women." He goes on to say that the reform movement did little more than displace the addicts from their palatial establishments in the Tenderloin and Chinatown to individual flats spread out over these and other areas of the city. In describing the difference between alcohol and opium, Crane becomes more than a reporter: "Billie Rostetter got drunk on whisky and emptied three scuttles of coal down the dumb-waiter shaft. This made a noise and Billy naturally was arrested. But opium is silent. These smokers do not rave. They lay and dream, or talk in low tones. The opium vice does not betray itself by heaving coal down dumb-waiter shafts" (8:366).

In this story, unlike most naturalists, Crane does not try to shock the reader. Instead, his incongruous analogies tend to be comical and are often the more penetrating because of ironic humor. The sickness that comes after one's first "pipe" is not described brutally or graphically. Rather, it is presented almost as a joke: "When a man arises from his first trial of the pipe, the nausea that clutches him is something that can give cards and spades and big casino to seasickness. If he had swallowed a live chimney-sweep he could not feel more like dying" (8:366). Notice the care taken in the choice of words; a chimney-sweep, of course, works in chimneys, and "pipes" are, of course, a kind of small chimney.

Only at the end does Crane editorialize in the manner of the social-reformer naturalist, and even then he does it intelligently and logically, and not with an eye on eliciting pity. Describing the effects of opium on the smoker as "a fine languor, a complete mental rest" (8:369), a mental state in which "wrong departs" and "injustice vanishes" (8:370), Crane then shifts his discussion from the specific to a more general class of people:

And who should invade the momentary land of rest, this dream country, if not the people of the Tenderloin, they who are at once supersensitive and hopeless, the people who think more upon death and the mysteries of life, the chances of the hereafter, than any other class, educated or uneducated. Opium holds out to them its lie, and they embrace it eagerly, expecting to find a definition of peace, but they awake to find the formidable labors of life grown more formidable. And if the pipe should happen to ruin their lives they cling to it the more closely because it stands between them and thought. (8:370)

Many naturalistic writers believed with Zola that society—or environment—was almost solely responsible for the plight of humanity, and that if the environment were changed for the better, people would be better.[17] Because the environment of the slums was degrading and evil, those who lived there were degraded and, usually, evil.

Crane had emerged from his "clever period" of the *Sullivan Cou ᵔⁱ Tales,* and while he still subscribed to his youthful belief in Howellsian realism, he could also write from an "activist" perspective. "In the Depths of A Coal Mine,"[18] journalistic and geographically removed from the Bowery, retains a perspective similar to that of his city tales. Written after a visit to an anthracite mine in Scranton, Pennsylvania, in June 1894, before Crane had become famous, the story describes the scene and Crane's feelings about a trip into the pits, a mile below ground. Despite the journalistic tone, the adjectives repeatedly remind the reader of hell. Young boys are "imps" (8:592), noises are "infernal" (8:593), the heads of two miners are "like the grinning of two skulls there in the shadows," movements are "shrouded," and the miners look like "spectres" (8:594).

Crane engages in some subtle editorializing as well: "If a [miner] can escape the gas, the floods, the 'squeezes' of falling rock, the cars shooting through little tunnels, the precarious elevators, the hundred perils, there usually comes to him an attack of 'miner's asthma' that slowly racks and shakes him into the grave. Meanwhile he gets three dollars a day, and his laborer one dollar and a quarter" (8:599). Given that unions were officially discouraged and generally feared by those in power, Crane had to be somewhat circumspect should he want to have his story published. He managed to find a way to convey the horror through analogy, apparently without offending. If these miners were "mules," there were also real mules to talk about. Mules were used to pull the coal carts and often remained in the tunnels for years.

Crane describes one mule, "our acquaintance, 'China', who had been buried for four years":

> Upon the surface there had been the march of the seasons; the white splendor of snows had changed again and again to the glories of spring greens. Four times had the earth been ablaze with the decorations of brilliant autumns. But "China" and his friends had remained in these dungeons from which daylight, if one could get a view up the shaft, would appear in a tiny circle, a silver star aglow in a sable sky.
>
> Usually when brought to the surface, these animals tremble at the earth, radiant in the sunshine. Later, they go almost mad with fantastic joy. The full splendor of the heavens, the grass, the trees, the breezes breaks upon them suddenly. They caper and career with extravagant mulish glee. . . .
>
> To those who have known the sunlight there may come the fragrant dream. Perhaps this is what they brood over when they stand solemnly in rows with slowly flapping ears. A recollection may appear to them, a recollection of pastures of a lost paradise. Perhaps they despair and thirst for this bloom that lies in an unknown direction and at impossible distances. (8:598–99)

What is true of mules may be true of the "mules" called miners.

That Crane modified his impressions is demonstrated by his first draft of this story, most of which survives.[19] In passages cut from the final draft, Crane casts aside analogy and editorializes directly about the cruelties of unbridled capitalism. He writes, "When I had studied mines and the miner's life underground and above ground, I wondered at many things but I could not induce myself to wonder why miners strike and otherwise object to their lot" (8:605). He savages some coalbrokers, those who buy and sell the coal dug from the earth, and who, in this instance, had been trapped for a while in a mine. Crane describes their rescue, and then adds the following: "If all men who stand uselessly and for their own extraordinary profit between the miner and the consumer were annually doomed to a certain period of danger and darkness in the mines, they might at last comprehend the misery and bitterness of men who toil for existence at these hopelessly grim tasks. They would begin to understand then the value of the miner, perhaps. Then maybe they would allow him a wage according to his part" (8:607).

It would be pleasant to believe that Crane was wholly in the grand

American tradition of literary social reformers, that he worked diligently to better conditions for the poor and downtrodden, and that he was indefatigable in his efforts to expose the cruelties and barbarisms of the powerful robber barons. The reality, however, is more complex and ambiguous. Nothing more clearly illustrates Crane's ambivalent attitude toward rich and poor than two companion pieces, "An Experiment in Misery" (8:283–93) and "An Experiment in Luxury" (8:293–301).

"An Experiment in Misery" is perhaps the most written about of the Bowery sketches. Its power derives not so much from the naturalistic or realistic quality of the narration, but rather from its imaginative, artistic vision of what hell must be like. The story opens with a young man, dressed in old and battered clothing, trudging from a "good" neighborhood to a "bad" one, in search of a flophouse. Finally, he finds a man who knows of one. The young man, clearly Crane out "experimenting" on Bowery life, follows the man, who looks like an "assassin," to a place that looks like a charnel house. He is led along "a dark street," up stairs, along a "gloom-shrouded corridor," to a door before a "black, opaque interior" (8:286–87). All this time, "strange and unspeakable odors . . . assailed him like malignant diseases with wings." When he enters the room, "unholy odors rushed out like released fiends" out of hell. Led to his bunk, a cold "slab," the youth sees lockers that look like tombstones, a gas jet that "burned a small flickering orange hued flame," and finally men "lying in death-like silence." A man in the next cot seems to be dead, as his eyes are open and he remains motionless all night.[20] In the darkness, the flophouse looks like hell: "all through the room could be seen the tawny hues of naked flesh, limbs thrust into the darkness, projecting beyond the cots; up-reared knees; arms hanging, long and thin, over the cot edges. For the most part, they were statuesque, carven, dead" (8:288).

The next morning, however, when the room seems "ordinary," the young man's guide expresses himself in ordinary terms. He fails to blame himself, blaming instead his father and a lack of work for his fate. He never sees his drinking as a cause of his miserable state. The sense of individual responsibility evident in this story is missing in most naturalistic fiction, but Crane does describe the incredible misery of these people in naturalistic terms, describing the hallucinatory screams and moans and shrieks of one sleeping man's utterances as symbolic "of the meaning of the room and its occupants . . . , giving voice to the wail of a whole section, a class, a people" (8:289). That the "assassin" and, presumably, most others, are contemptible does not blind Crane to their condition. Their condition, on the other hand, does not blind him to their contemptibleness.

"An Experiment in Luxury" takes the same young man from the flophouse to the mansion. A young man on his way to "make a study" of millionaires meets an older friend who sets the stage by debunking the accepted prattle about how wealth makes people unhappy. He suggests that wealth is built on "robbery," recalling George Bernard Shaw's comment that behind every great fortune lies a great crime. The youth will hear none of this, and refuses to believe that the rich friend coming to take him to dinner at home ever robbed anyone. When he arrives at the mansion, however, the young man is disappointed; it looks "like the face of a peasant . . . , rugged, grimly self-reliant asserting its quality as a fine thing when in reality the beholder usually wondered why so much money had been spent to obtain a complete negation" (8:295). The footman is described as one "who must be more atrociously aristocratic than any that he serves." Inside, and in contrast to the little gas flame in the flophouse, there is "an immense fire" in an "amazingly comfortable room" (8:296).

During a conversation with his college friend, "he began to see a vast wonder in it that the two lay sleepily chatting with no more apparent responsibility than rabbits, when certainly there were men, equally fine perhaps, who were being blackened and mashed in the churning life of the lower places" (8:297). Looking around, the youth becomes affected by the trappings of wealth: "He stretched his legs like a man in a garden, and he thought that he belonged to the garden. . . . He was become a philosopher, a type of wise man who can eat but three meals a day, conduct a large business and understand the purposes of infinite power. He felt valuable. He was sage and important" (8:297). He sees the millionaire playing with a kitten, deep in universal emotions "in a far land . . . , a mystic little land" (8:298). His wife, on the other hand, was "a savage, a barbarian, a spear woman of the Philistines" (8:299). His friend's three sisters "were wonderful to him in their charming gowns. They had time and opportunity to create effects, to be beautiful. And it would have been a wonder to him if he had not found them charming, since making themselves so could but be their principal occupation" (8:300). At dinner, the conversation is banal, which was not "what the youth had been taught to see. Theologians had for a long time told the poor man that riches did not bring happiness, and they had solemnly repeated this phrase until it had come to mean that misery was commensurate with dollars. . . . And when a wail of despair or rage had come from the night of the slums they had stuffed this epigram down the throat of he who cried out and told him that he was a lucky fellow" (8:301).

"An Experiment in Misery" is a cold, hard look at slums and slum-dwellers. "An Experiment in Luxury" is a brutal, savage attack on the rich. Crane was on nobody's "side" politically, if that "side" included more than one person. He did once come to the aid of a prostitute wrongly accused of soliciting. And by testifying on her behalf in open court, Crane besmirched his name and was virtually driven from New York City. This, as much as anything else, made him part of another grand American literary tradition: the American expatriate in Europe.

The truth is that Crane kept a wary eye out for "isms"; he distrusted anything that explained everything. Regarding socialism, for example, Crane was explicit, albeit jokingly so: "I was a socialist for two weeks, but when a couple of Socialists assured me that I had no right to think differently from any other Socialist and then quarreled with each other about what Socialism meant, I ran away."[21]

Although sympathetic to the plight of slum-dwellers, Crane could also be hard on them. "The root of Bowery life," he once said, "is a sort of cowardice."[22] It may be that Crane partook of what Fredric Jameson calls "the primal nineteenth-century middle-class terror of the mob."[23] Or, it may be that Crane simply distrusted the motives of groups. In his view, coming directly from the rationalist tradition, only individuals can even attempt to see, to perceive, to understand; groups cannot. Consequently, to assert that groups can do anything that Crane considered important is to undermine his most deeply held beliefs.

Such views are far more existential than naturalistic. While sharing with naturalism a belief in a motiveless, chaotic universe, existential-ism posits a different attitude. Precisely because humanity is the product of chance, precisely because there is no purpose guiding life, individuals are free, utterly free, to make their own choices. It is ex-istential, then, to see the individual as isolated from the environment, rather than subsumed in it. The social-reformer naturalist does not say such things as Crane said about the Bowery. And, indeed, during the social upheaval of the 1930s, several critics expressed disdain for Crane, considering his writings politically and socially "incorrect."[24] On the other hand, such are the complexities and ambiguities of Crane's fiction that some critics, as late as the 1950s, were still providing tortured, gross misreadings to make him speak for Marxism.[25]

The quality that most separates Crane from the confines of naturalism, however, is the richness of his genius. It could not be contained adequately in narrow theories. Many critics, of course, have chosen to emphasize Crane's other, often contradictory themes and methods. But Milne Holton, in *Cylinder of Vision*, was among the first to attack directly and thoroughly the notion of Crane as a naturalist. Holton showed that virtually all of Crane's characters are isolated from their environments, and seem bound by no natural laws of heredity or environment.[26] The correspondent, for example, could not be farther from his normal surroundings than when rowing for his life in a tiny dinghy on the cold, January waters of the Atlantic. Other such characters, not yet discussed, populate many of Crane's stories. Scratchy Wilson, in "The Bride Comes to Yellow Sky," is completely out of his element in facing down an unarmed and married lawman. In "The Blue Hotel," the Swede, a fearful, urban tailor, is in a "splendor of isolation" as he tears the seams out of the Nebraska blizzard. Doctor Trescott, in "The Monster," is an honorable man struggling hopelessly against the thoroughly dishonorable community of Whilomville. And the protagonists of the later war stories are ordinary folk, far from the routines of their everyday lives, forced to endure the utterly unfamiliar surroundings and frightening events of the booming chaos of war, and yet sufficiently strong to remain, in most cases, themselves. Even in Crane's most famous "naturalistic" novel, the protagonist, Maggie, is a "flower" that "blossomed in a mud puddle." Because this quality contradicts a central tenet of naturalism, namely that environment dictates the way people are, Crane cannot be a naturalist.

In Crane's nihilism there also lies an element of existentialism that implies that each individual is condemned to live as a momentary flash in the encompassing darkness of the universe, that life is meaningless to the universe, but also that each individual is therefore free to make choices. Meaningless or not, these choices make us human, and distinguish us from other living creatures. The implication is that human beings have an obligation, if they want to be human, to make moral choices. Silly, even ridiculous, qualities such as honor and justice and individual morality are important for they are all we have. If life is meaningless, then life is free. If life is free, we can make some of it what we will. And, for Crane, the making of it is important.

Tales of the West and Mexico

Having gained some notoriety with newspaper people for his sketches in and around New York City, for *Maggie* with William Dean Howells and Hamlin Garland, and for the manuscript of *The Red Badge* with publisher Irving Bacheller, Crane persuaded the Bacheller Syndicate to take a chance on sending him west to write a series of articles on conditions there, especially of the long drought in the prairie. After much delay, Crane finally left New York in January 1895, and, travelling by rail through Philadelphia and Chicago, he arrived in St. Louis by 30 January. From there he went to Omaha and to Lincoln, where he met Willa Cather, then a young reporter. In early February, he was caught in a blizzard in Eddyville, a little town in north central Nebraska. By 20 February, he was in New Orleans. Then, in March, he went west to Texas and Mexico. By mid-May, he was home again.

If Crane's western sojourn had provided the experience necessary for his writing nothing more than "The Bride Comes to Yellow Sky" and "The Blue Hotel," that would have been sufficient for literary history. But there was much more. Crane now had a wealth of experience about which to write. The blizzard he saw in Nebraska resulted immediately in a justly famous journalistic piece called "Nebraska's Bitter Fight for Life,"[27] published in February 1895; later, in 1898, he wrote "The Blue Hotel." He saw Hot Springs, Arkansas; New Orleans; Galveston; San Antonio; and Mexico. All of these places provided inspiration for writing: "Seen at Hot Springs" (8:420–25), "Grand Opera in New Orleans" (8:425–29), "The City of Mexico" (8:429–32), "The Viga Canal" (8:432–35), "The Mexican Lower Classes" (8:435–38), "Stephen Crane in Mexico: I" (8:438–44), "Stephen Crane in Mexico: II" (8:446–56), "Free Silver Down in Mexico" (8:444–46), "A Jug of Pulque Is Heavy" (8:456–59), "Hats, Shirts, and Spurs in Mexico" (8:465–68), "Stephen Crane in Texas" (8:468–74), and "Galveston, Texas, in 1895" (8:474–79).

Crane saw that the West was not the "Wild West" of his imagination, but an "Easternized" West. In fact, much of his western writing describes this change in terms of an invasion of migrants from the Eastern states that occurred throughout the second half of the nineteenth century. Characteristically, Crane turns this invasion to ironic effect. In "The Bride Comes to Yellow Sky," for example, Crane makes clear that the "new" (Eastern society and values) that replaces the "old" (Western society and values) is not quite the fresh, young, boundlessly hopeful generation or society usually associated with comedy, even in an essentially comic tale. In "The Bride Comes to Yellow Sky," the archetypal comedy of "The Pace of Youth" is inverted: the generation being replaced is "newer" and "fresher," and, as Crane said, more "honest" than the one replacing it.

"The Bride" illustrates a new maturity in Crane that moves beyond the purely archetypal comedy related in "The Pace of Youth," in which history plays no part. In "The Bride," history becomes integral to the meaning. Potter represents the new West—domesticated, law-abiding, and relatively tame—and, as he is riding the train, he is associated with that symbol of the East and of civilization. Scratchy Wilson represents the old Wild West, rambling, untamed, isolated. He is like the wild, winding river near which he used to live: "He's about the last one of the old gang that used to hang out along the river here" (5:116).

The story's first paragraph displays an impressionistic trick of the eye and mind. To the eye, "The great Pullman was whirling onward with such dignity of motion that a glance from the window seemed simply to prove that the plains of Texas were pouring eastward" (5:109). Actually, we think more often of the "East," the civilized, domestic East, moving toward, even invading the West. The mind, as well as the eye, is tricked here. It is interesting to note also the speed with which this is occurring. Northern Europeans had lived on the North American continent for about two centuries before they finally crossed the Mississippi River in any numbers. Yet the West was settled almost entirely in the forty years after 1850.

For a long time, critics viewed "The Bride Comes to Yellow Sky" (5:109–20) as a parody, and *only* a parody, of the kind of Western originally portrayed in the cheap dime novels of Crane's day, old movies like *High Noon*, and continued by such contemporary popular writers as Louis L'Amour, and a host of television Westerns. Edwin Cady, for example, wrote in 1961 that "The Bride" is "a hilariously funny parody of the neo-romantic lamentations over 'The Passing of the West.' "[28] Indeed, the method is that of mock epics: laughter derives from the surprise at perceiving the difference between expectations of heroic deeds and of performance decidedly mundane. "The Bride," in short, scoops the movie *Blazing Saddles* by about eighty years.

The parodic method of "The Bride" is that of reversing the normal expectation of readers. "The Bride" takes the comic plot of boy meets girl and so on and changes the standard order in which we expect comedy to proceed; in fact, the opposite of our expectations occurs. "The Bride" begins with the hero, Marshall Jack Potter, riding westward, not on a horse, but in a train. Marriage—rarely achieved in standard Westerns—has occurred before the story opens, and the marshall and his bride are, in fact, probably on what is passing for their honeymoon. In addition, neither the marshall nor his bride is quite what is expected. The marshall appears to be out of his element on the train: "The man's face was reddened from many days in the wind and sun, and a direct result of his new black clothes was that his brick-colored hands were constantly performing in a most conscious fashion. He sat with a hand on each knee, like a man waiting in a barber's shop" (5:109). The bride, unlike the desert roses of standard Westerns, "was not pretty nor was she very young" (5:109). Neither is she the daughter of some wealthy rancher fallen on hard times: "It was quite apparent that she had cooked, and that she expected to cook, dutifully" (5:109).

Section 2 of "The Bride" introduces the third major character: outlaw Scratchy Wilson, who is simultaneously the most comic and most tragic character in the story. Before he appears, Scratchy is described by a citizen of Yellow Sky to a newcomer. The reader and the newcomer are told that "There'll be some shootin'—some good shootin' ": Scratchy, "a wonder with a gun," "is drunk and has turned loose with both hands," (5:114) ready to shoot indiscriminately at doors, dogs, windows, houses, and, presumably, people. Crane leads the reader to believe that the expectations of the standard Western will be fulfilled: wild and deadly Scratchy Wilson is going to do something wild and deadly. Scratchy's actual performance is wild, but, in the end, hardly deadly. His marksmanship leaves much to be desired: he misses the dog, and he misses a paper target nailed to the barroom door. Moreover, he grossly violates readers' expectations: when he finally comes face-to-face with the marshall, Scratchy drops his revolver in the dirt. Gunfighters may be many things, but they may not be clumsy. The point of this, of course, is to poke fun not so much at Scratchy Wilson as at the standard Western and at the reader who expects a standard Western.

While most of its action reverses the order of the formula Western, "The Bride" does accept the Western's typical movement toward a "showdown" (or, more properly, "walkdown"). Crane demonstrates complete control over prefiguring, which occurs early in "The Bride." Although the walkdown is the climax of the story, the reader is provided a verbal and symbolic map of the area at the story's beginning: "To the left, miles down a long purple slope, was a little ribbon of mist where moved the keening Rio Grande" (5:111). Graphically, the movements of Potter and Scratchy toward a walkdown may be plotted as two intersecting lines: when they cross, the walkdown occurs. The outcome of the meeting on the dusty streets of Yellow Sky is much more than parodic. If Potter represents the "New" West and Scratchy the Old West, then the prefiguring at the story's beginning allows the walkdown to be thought of as a confrontation between the new "civilized" West—the railroad, law and order, and domestic institutions such as marriage—and the old, "Wild" West. In the tradition of mock-epic, the defeat of Scratchy Wilson does not end in the roar and smoke of blazing pistols. In fact, when Potter says to Wilson, "I ain't got a gun on me, Scratchy," Wilson is nonplussed: "If you ain't got a gun, why ain't you got a gun? . . . Been to Sunday-school?" (5:119). A gunfight in which only one participant is armed violates the formula. Scratchy may be dastardly, but he is not evil. Then, as if to add insult to injury, Potter informs Wilson of his marriage: "'Married!'" says Scratchy. "He was not a student of chivalry. . . . He picked up his starboard revolver, and . . . he went away. His feet made funnel-shaped tracks in the heavy sand" (5:120). Skillfully using comedy, irony, parody, and even geometry, Crane creates a perfect architecture, the nonparallel lines of the funnel-shaped tracks, like those of the railroad and the river, meeting and disappearing in the sands of West Texas. The Old West dies not with a bang, but with a whimper.

In one of Crane's most famous stories, "The Blue Hotel" (5:142–70), the Old West, at least as it exists in the mind of the Swede, dies with a bang. The story is also a fine example of Crane's use of formal tragedy. The setting is Fort Romper, a prairie town, in the late 1800s. Chaos is represented by a storm so severe that the narrator remarks that "conceit is the very engine of life." Order is represented, as often in Crane, by a stove.[29] In "The Blue Hotel," the stove hums away in the Palace Hotel, and all descending levels of order move outward from it. The stove is surrounded by several guests; the room surrounding the guests is the social center of the hotel: "The room . . . was small. It seemed to be merely a proper temple for an enormous stove, which, in the center, was humming with god-like violence" (5:143). The hotel is an expression of ego and order, a worthy antagonist to the chaos of nature represented by a mindless, indifferent blizzard surrounding the hotel: "The Palace Hotel at Fort Romper was painted a light blue, a shade that is on the legs of a kind of heron, causing the bird to declare its position against any background" (5:142).

Into this scene comes a train. And from this train disembarks "a shaky and quick-eyed Swede" (5:143). He is shaky because he "has been reading dime-novels, and he thinks he's right out in the middle of it—shootin' and stabbin' and all" (5:153). By 1890, the frontier officially was gone in America, and innkeeper Scully says, "Why, man, we're goin' to have a line of ilitric street-cars in this town next spring" (5:149). To the Swede, on the other hand, Fort Romper remains the Wild West, and he announces to the group: "I'm crazy—yes. But I know one thing. . . . I know I won't get out of here alive" (5:147). Persuaded to stay, the Swede plays cards with other guests and with Johnnie, Scully's son. That Johnnie probably cheats at cards is made evident in the first scene in the hotel; a disgusted farmer storms away from a card game with Johnnie. Later, the Swede accuses Johnnie of cheating, and finally, the Easterner admits to seeing Johnnie cheat. Still, after his accusation, the Swede is forced to fight. Although the group cheers for Johnnie, the Swede wins. Inflated by his victory, the Swede strides to a different part of town, enters a bar, picks on a gambler, and is stabbed to death.

Part of the story's greatness lies in the levels of misperception about order and chaos that stem from Johnnie's cheating on the one hand and the Swede's admitted insanity on the other. In early stories like "Uncle Jake and the Bell-Handle" and "The Mesmeric Mountain," misperceptions are simple and one-dimensional. The protagonists simply see order and purpose where there is none. In "The Blue Hotel," however, misperceptions are more complex. Every character misperceives, either seeing order where there is none or participating in a kind of order that merely suspends chaos. The best example of this suspension or deferral of chaos is the conspiracy of silence among the other hotel guests. Even the reader is often misled, and, in fact, is offered several ways to perceive the truth. For the reader, one major question is this: Is the Swede crazy or does he perceive the truth? It is usually assumed that the Swede is crazy, not only because he says so himself, but also because the others seem not to understand the source of the Swede's

outrageous statements. For example, when the Swede asks, "I suppose there have been a good many men killed in this room" (5:146),
the cowboy pretends not to know what is going on, Johnnie says he
does not know what the Swede is talking about, and the Easterner,
"after prolonged and cautious reflection," replies to the Swede, "I
don't understand you." If he is crazy and Johnnie is not cheating, then
the Swede's own misperception leads to the fight. Conversely, if the
"quick-eyed Swede" is not crazy or is crazy in a way different from
common insanity—that is, if he is indeed perceptive, if the earlier
quarrel between the farmer and Johnnie involved cheating, and if the
Swede understood the reason for the quarrel—then the misperceptions
are of a different kind. Either the others do not see Johnnie cheating
or they deliberately ignore it. If the latter, then the comments of the
others may indeed be seen by a sane man as a conspiracy: "you are all
against me," says the Swede.

If the scene leading from the second card game between Johnnie
and the farmer and to the Swede's "three terrible words: 'You are
cheating!' " (5:156), is read as one in which the Swede actually sees
Johnnie cheating, then he may be excused for believing himself to be
in a dangerous place: the Wild West where card games end with cheating exposed and murder imposed. The Swede watches the card game
until "the play of Johnnie and the [farmer] was suddenly ended with
another quarrel" (5:145). Casting "heated scorn" on Johnnie, the
farmer leaves the room. Then, "in the discreet silence of the other
men, the Swede laughed" (5:145). Next, the Swede plays with Johnnie, the cowboy, and the Easterner. Making remarks about men being
killed, the Swede notes that the others either ignore or dismiss what
he says. When the cowboy asks, "Say, what are you gittin' at hey?" the
Swede springs up and shouts, "I don't want to fight" (5:146). Trying
to calm the Swede, Scully invites him to have a drink. Afraid to drink
and afraid not to drink, the Swede does so, but looks "with hatred" at
Scully. Although the reader does not know how much the Swede
drinks, it is clearly too much, for at dinner "the Swede fizzed like a
firewheel." His reluctance becomes belligerence, and he dominates
others in the room. He accepts Johnnie's challenge to another game,
only to end it by accusing Johnnie of cheating.

In the Wild West of our and the Swede's imagination, that would
have been an end. Johnnie would have drawn a six-gun, said "Smile
when you say that, stranger," and then shot the Swede. That this does
not happen derives from two other levels of misperception. First, the

"screaming" contrast between the electric blue of the Palace Hotel and the blinding white Nebraska landscape mentioned in the story's first paragraph represents an important contrast between order and chaos.[30] Scully's hotel observes a kind of order that stands out from the surrounding chaos of the blizzard. The hotel, with the stove, the "rules" of conduct (Scully prohibits anyone ganging up on the Swede), and what Weinig calls a "patriarchal household . . . whose ceremonious hospitality . . . brooks no violation,"[31] is a model of order in this "ice-locked" world. The Swede misperceives the hotel as a chaotic place. Second, he again misperceives when he leaves the hotel and finds a bar. He assumes that the rules are the same in the bar as in the hotel. They are not, and he dies as a result.

It may be difficult to see the Swede as a tragic hero, for he does not seem to have the great stature granted to traditional heroes. But in a democracy, heroes, tragic or otherwise, are usually of the common folk, and the Swede is a tailor. Moreover, the Swede does not arrive on the scene fully formed as a tragic hero. Rather, like most of Crane's heroes, he must first discover the meaning of heroism and then act upon that discovery. The first half of "The Blue Hotel," then, may be seen as leading to the Swede's commitment to action. When he arrives at the hotel and sees Johnnie cheating, he has to decide to call him on it. Somewhere between taking the drink offered by Scully and insisting on another game with Johnnie, the Swede makes his decision to say "You are cheating!" With these words, the Swede becomes, in a bizarre way, a hero. That is, armed with the truth, a determination to side with honesty, and a decision to defy the others as classical heroes defy the gods, he dominates. He dominates the entire table at dinner. Significantly, "He seemed to have grown suddenly taller. . . . His voice rang through the whole room" (5:154) and he nearly harpoons the Easterner's hand with a fork while both are reaching for a biscuit. By beating Johnnie in the fight, the Swede clearly has won. He has asserted his will, his vision of honesty, and dominated the blue hotel and everyone in it. Such an act, especially against the five men's conspiracy to ignore dishonesty, may be seen as an heroic act. But by so doing, he is exiled, as all tragic heroes finally are, to "a splendor of isolation" (5:161).

Having risen to such heights in this tragedy, the Swede can only go down. And he does, quickly, because he believes that he is indomitable and that the rest of the universe plays by the same rules. Filled with a sense "of conquering and elate humanity," the Swede oversteps the boundaries of the Palace Hotel, marches into the storm, and finds a saloon quite unlike the hotel. Attempting to assert himself as he had in the hotel, the Swede is killed, and with his death comes a recognition of fragile mortality, of the fleeting nature of heroism: this man, says the narrator, "this citadel of virtue, wisdom, power [is] pierced as easily as if it had been a melon" (5:168–69). The Swede's dead eyes are "fixed upon a dreadful legend that dwelt a-top of the cash-machine. 'This registers the amount of your purchase.' "

That amount must have read "$0.00," for the only kind of formal tragedy possible for Crane is derived from delusion. Heroes cannot embody the mythic stature required to keep whole nations secure under the brow of their eagle-eyed prowess. Heroes can only imagine such a world, and even then, only briefly fulfill the requirements of their own imaginations before falling victim to a group of lesser men. When the Easterner acknowledges his part in the conspiracy, he says also "We're all in it" (5:170). Even the Swede, marching into the storm, counts cadence to his own quick march to doom. The Swede is possessed, indeed, but perhaps by something inhuman and ineluctable. A drummer-boy to the fates, he alone hears their tune. Those who hear it, too, but who fail to act, like the Easterner, are cowards. All this derives from a card game, a small ritual played out in Nebraska. Still, rituals are important to Crane. To act honestly is one way to find meaning in a meaningless world, and, for Crane, the Swede found that meaning, if only momentarily, before losing it somewhere between the hotel and the saloon.

It should be remembered that "The Bride" and "The Blue Hotel" are the comic and tragic faces of the same misperception: Scratchy finds that the rules of society have changed; the Swede, first in the hotel, thinks they have when they have not, and then, in the saloon, that they have not when indeed they have. In this way the two stories are companion pieces, and looked at in this way, they shed light on a remark made by the narrator in "The Blue Hotel": "Any room can present a tragic front; any room can be comic" (5:156).

If "The Bride Comes to Yellow Sky" and "The Blue Hotel" are Crane's two best Western stories, he did write others, like "Moonlight on the Snow," "Twelve O'Clock," "The Wise Men: A Detail of American Life in Mexico," "The Five White Mice," "One Dash—Horses," "A Man and Some Others," that just miss greatness. None of these stories is as perfect as "The Bride" or "The Blue Hotel": sometimes the narrative intrusion is too great, too insistent and strident; some lack the unity of "The Bride"; and, some, like "The Wise Men" and "The Five White Mice," are too long and filled with youthful spirits to sustain the nihilism of the theme of chance. Yet the indifferent landscape remains, the exile from reality still appears in that landscape, the instinctive groping toward ritual is made manifest, and two conflicts still form the central concerns of these stories: the outward conflict between the individual and the group and the inward mental turmoil between illusory notions of an idealized West filled with rugged individualists and the overlying reality of an encroaching Eastern civilization that values conformity. The juxtaposition of the old and the new, the "primitive" and the "civilized," is a catalyst, the mere presence of which excites these conflicts.

With the coming of Eastern values, the Old West's concern for survival capitulates easily to a new concern for capital. If the Palace Hotel exists, in part, to mediate between the harsh Nebraska environment and Easterners, it also exists to glean money from railway passengers. In "Moonlight on the Snow" (5:180–91), the citizens of War Post are concerned that the violence visible everywhere in "wild" towns will shut off the imaginary spigot of capital that they believe will pour money into the land near town. This concern for money derives in part from the belief that by amassing wealth people can remove themselves further from the violent reality so apparent in the land. War Post is a town famous for its Wild-West, shoot-first-ask-questions-later, citizens. Because land speculators have moved into the area, all the nearby "tame" towns are making money, while War Post "ain't yit seen a centavo" (5:180–81). Consequently, "War Post resolved to be virtuous" by decreeing "that no man should kill another man under penalty of being at once hanged by the populace" (5:181).

The next morning, Tom Larpent, a leading citizen and a gambler who "had been educated somewhere," shoots another man for accusing him of cheating at cards and for being "officious. Not enough men are shot on that account" (5:183). The populace wants Larpent hanged because, as Larpent himself says, "the value of human life must be established before there can be theatres, water-works, street-cars, women and babies" (5:180). Larpent must be hanged simply as a matter of economics: "It's all well enough to set 'round takin' money from innercent cowpunchers a'long's ther's nothin' better; but when these here speculators come 'long flashin' rolls as big as water-buckets, it's up to us to whirl in an' git some of it" (5:180).

With the exception of Doctor Trescott in the Whilomville stories,

Tom Larpent is perhaps the most sophisticated of Crane's protagonists. As such, to the citizens of War Post, he may be a trifle suspect, and therefore more easily sacrificed by War Post on the altar of Money. Larpent is, after all, already an entrepreneur, and his gambling house is "the biggest institution in War Post." He secretly imports whisky from the East, is among those who assent to the new "hanging" law, and reads Sir Walter Scott. A complicated man, Larpent becomes the mouthpiece for Crane's familiar denigration of dogma and a "civilization" personified by clergymen and bartenders. The first tend to be self-satisfied prigs, and the latter are often mere spineless money-counters, attributes often leading them to become community leaders. In "Moonlight on the Snow," the position of clergyman is filled by Mister Simpson, who is, "on occasion, the voice of the town. Somewhere in his past he had been a Baptist preacher, [but] he had fallen far, very far, and the only remnant of his former dignity was a fatal facility of speech when half drunk" (5:183). Croaking "like a frog," Simpson attempts to elicit a confession from Larpent, when Larpent interrupts by asserting that "officious" men deserve to be shot: "As one fitted in every way to be consummately officious, I hope you will agree, Mr. Simpson." The bartender, Bobbie Hether, receives a similar tongue-lashing as Larpent is being led to the rope: "I am resolved to devote my inquiries as to the welfare of my friends. Now, you, for instance, my dear Bobbie, present today the lamentable appearance of a rattlesnake that has been four times killed and then left to rot in the sun" (5:184).

When a stage coach rattles into town, Larpent is saved from the gallows. The citizens fear that, should a speculator be aboard, the sight of a hanging on the town's main street would confirm him in the general opinion of War Post as being unworthy of receiving capital. As the coach contains no speculators, but rather "a beautiful young woman," "two little girls," and "a white-haired old gentleman," the citizens are perplexed. "As the illumined eyes of the girl wandered doubtfully, fearfully, toward the man with the rope around his neck, a certain majority of the practiced ruffians tried to look as if they were having nothing to do with the proceedings" (5:185). Larpent is saved, left alone to sit on some steps. That he still has the rope around his neck attests not only to Larpent's unconcern, but also to the power of Eastern women and the civilization they represent. The citizens forget their purpose and fail to remove the evidence of it.

Once again Sheriff Jack Potter and his deputy, Scratchy Wilson, making their only appearance in Crane's fiction other than in "The Bride Comes to Yellow Sky," contribute to the anticlimax. They have come to arrest Larpent for grand larceny, a charge of which he will be acquitted, no doubt, for no one in War Post will testify against him. Everyone wins except the dead man shot by Larpent, and the tenderfoot who brought the charges. Larpent will be free and War Post will gain respectability for having obeyed the law.

"Moonlight on the Snow" misses greatness for two reasons. First, Larpent, in his bitterly ironical comments about his fellow citizens and their motives of greed, is too much a jaded mouthpiece of the views of the narrator, and second, the story's anticlimax—Larpent's act of sitting on the steps with the rope still around his neck—is a bit overdone. "The Bride's" ending is perfect; that of "Moonlight on the Snow" is not.

"Twelve O'Clock" (5:171–78) is another tale of old and new, wild and civilized. At least one man dies and another is wounded in a strange, drunken gathering of cowboys who come to see a cuckoo clock at Placer's Hotel. When the cuckoo emerges from a clock to announce eleven o'clock, a cowboy is amazed, having never before seen such a thing. When he tells his friends about the clock, even those who know about cuckoo clocks accuse him of having hallucinations from bad whisky, and so he persuades them to go to the hotel to see for themselves. When they arrive, dangerous arguments ensue, prompting an inoffensive hotel clerk, Placer (Placid?), to come out from behind the counter, level two pistols at the group and warn them to take their fight outside. One cowboy, Big Watson, laughs and shoots Placer through the throat. Pandemonium breaks out, a cowboy in the street is shot accidentally, and Jake hits Big Watson over the head. As they carry Watson away, the cuckoo appears from the clock and cries " 'Cuckoo'—twelve times."

It is sometimes said that people looking for a fight—or an "assassin," as one of Crane's poems puts it—will find it. Curiously, this clock, a symbol of Eastern civilization, is an entirely passive agent in causing the deaths of people who were not looking for a fight. In any clash between civilizations there is insanity and usually death, and, as "cuckoo" is a colloquialism for "crazy," the clock, like the cash register in "The Blue Hotel," comments on the meaning of those events, the amount of their purchase, which, in a world of chance, is that people pay with their lives for nothing.

"The Wise Men: A Detail of American Life in Mexico" (8:26–38)

And "The Five White Mice" (8:39–52) can be considered companion pieces, for the main characters are the same; and together the stories examine two results of two games of chance.[32] Ultimately, one is reminded that for all the games that humans play, chance rules in bigger games as well. In the first piece, "The Wise Men," two "Kids," one from New York and the other from San Francisco, engage in high jinks of the kind Crane might have indulged in had he had money or, perhaps, had he won a sufficient number of bets while he was in Mexico City. The two young Americans bet that an out-of-shape and presumably middle-aged bartender named "Pop," who used to be a sprinter of some note, can outrun a younger, slimmer bartender named Freddy. Many people misperceive Pop as incapable of beating Freddy in a 100-yard dash, and so the two young men have many takers. They have so many bets on the race that both get "in pretty deep," in "deep as the devil." Fortunately for the two Kids, Pop wins. Were it not for "The Five White Mice," which provides a counterpoint, "The Wise Men" would have little point, other than that of dumb luck making an ironical comment on the "wisdom" mentioned in the title.

"The Five White Mice" refers to the "five white mice of chance" chanted by the New York Kid in a game using five dice. Unlike the two Kids in "The Wise Men," the New York Kid loses at dice, and consequently he must take the winners to the circus. As no prudent person would bet on an over-the-hill bartender, the results of both games are equally ruled by chance. After the circus, he meets the San Francisco Kid and Benson, who have been drinking heavily. When the three Americans pass three Mexicans on a street, another game of chance occurs, another ritual in the clash of cultures, only this time the stakes are very high. Benson accidentally bumps one of the Mexicans in passing. As in typical Westerns, there is a confrontation. One Mexican says, "Does the señor want fight?" Before the New York Kid can say anything, Benson answers with a drunken "Yes!"

The three Mexicans and the three Americans pair off, seemingly nose to nose. The situation is, as they say, very serious: the Mexicans have knives, and the Americans have pistols, but, in the slow hands of the San Francisco Kid and Benson, the guns are useless. Even the New York Kid, the only sober American, is concerned and frightened. He knows that should he draw his pistol, he would have to do so very quickly. Any hitch in the holster would make him too slow, resulting perhaps in his death and those of his friends. Nevertheless, he draws. Fortunately, the pistol comes out smoothly and he gets "the drop" on the Mexicans. This done, one Mexican says, "Well, señor, it is finished?" The Kid answers, "I am willing." The Mexicans leave. The two drunks, unaware of the seriousness of the situation, move away with their savior. The story ends ironically. The drunks upbraid the New York Kid for losing at dice, which prevented him from joining them earlier to get drunk: "Kid shober 'cause didn't go with us. Didn't go with us 'cause went to damn circus. Went to damn circus 'cause lose shakin' dice. Lose shakin' dice 'cause—what make lose shakin' dice, Kid?" (8:52) By losing at dice, he won their lives. In a world where losing may be winning and winning losing, chance rules, indeed. Moreover, the Kid's chant about the five white mice may be seen as a ritualistic response to the intuitive knowledge that chance rules in a chaotic universe.

These stories help to explain the importance of self-control in situations ruled by chance. In "The Wise Men," the Kids may bet far more on Pop than they can afford to lose, because they remain outwardly controlled and calm—a kind of ritualized behavior: one simply "behaves well"—and because they are aided by chance, they win a lot of money. The sobriety maintained by the New York Kid in "The Five White Mice" occurs purely by chance (he lost at dice), but his control not only contrasts with the drunkenness, and therefore lack of control, of the other two Americans in "The Five White Mice," but also clearly saves their lives.

Two other stories, "One Dash—Horses" (5:13–25) and "A Man and Some Others" (5:53–67), also involve winning and losing, self-control, and chance. In the first, an American named Richardson and a Mexican named José, thoroughly exhausted and hungry from days in the Mexican desert, arrive at an isolated village. The poverty and consequent envy of the people become apparent after Richardson enters the cantina: "The woman . . . gazed at his enormous silver spurs, his large and impressive revolver, with the interest and admiration of the highly privileged cat of the adage" (5:14). Richardson is nearly asleep when he is aroused by "the sound of a guitar. It was badly played. . . ." The noise continues and grows louder. He hears men arguing, and then sees a "blanket hanging flat against the wall at the further end of the room." Realizing that the blanket may conceal a doorway, he "pulled his revolver closer to him and prepared for sudden disaster" (5:15). He falls asleep again, but is wakened by angry words coming from behind the blanket: "Yes, I will kill him! Listen! I will ask the American beast for his beautiful pistol and spurs and money and saddle, and if he will not give them—you will see!ᵞ Richardson is frightened, naturally: "his knee-joints turned to bread." Soon, a drunken Mexican, with five or six of his companions, enters Richardson's room. Richardson's refusal to respond to their insults, beyond staring, disconcerts the Mexican, but a showdown seems imminent. But suddenly distracted by the sound of women's laughter in the other room, the Mexicans leave to join the women.

Once again, a protagonist is saved from death by chance, in this instance the fortuitous timing of the women's arrival. After much carousing, the Mexicans fall asleep. Richardson waits and stares at the blanket, but finally dozes off. Awaking before dawn and before the Mexicans, Richardson flees with José. Soon, however, the Mexicans start after them: "Richardson, again looking backward, could see a slanting flare of dust on the whitening plain. He thought he could detect small figures moving in it." The outlaws begin to close the gap, for, while Richardson's horse continues to perform well, José's big black horse begins to flag. Richardson slows. The Mexicans close sufficiently to be heard shouting and to fire a shot. Chance enters again as Richardson and José happen across the Federales, "that crack cavalry corps of the Mexican army which polices the land so zealously . . ." (5:23). In all the vast space of the Mexican plain, the odds of running into the police are not good. Richardson was lucky. He was lucky, too, in having a strong and spirited horse.

Luck is certainly a theme of the story, but so, too, is the notion of veiled reality. The blanket behind which the outlaws drink and dance becomes a metaphor both for humanity's extremely limited understanding of reality and for fear of death. Knowledge of that limitation and suspicion that death waits behind the blanket bring fear:

> The blanket over the door fascinated him. It was a vague form, black and unmoving. Through the door was to come, probably, threats, death. Sometimes he thought he saw it move. As grim white sheets, the black and silver of coffins, all the panoply of death, affect us because of what they hide, so this blanket, dangling before a hole in an adobe wall, was to Richardson a horrible emblem, and horrible in itself. In his present mood, Richardson could not have been brought to touch it with his finger (5:18).

Like the Kids in Mexico City, Richardson survives by a combination of luck, self-control, and sobriety. Once again, Crane takes a protagonist to the edge of fear, creates circumstances that place chaos (the drunken Mexicans) and order (self-imposed by the protagonist) in opposition, and demonstrates that even great self-control is not enough for survival. Had the Federales not arrived, Richardson and José were doomed.

"A Man and Some Others" has several things in common with "One Dash—Horses": sheer chance, the apprehension of reality in danger and death, the cowardly bravado of groups, and the tenacity with which some people do what they do, all the while knowing the dire consequences. The protagonist of this story, however, is not so lucky. Chance and a certain bullheaded tenacity have brought a former Wyoming mine owner named Bill to the West Texas plains as a shepherd. He had been a cowboy, a brakeman for the Union Pacific, a strikebreaker, and a bouncer for a bar in New York's Bowery. He lost the mine in a card game, his job as cowboy for killing the foreman, and his job in New York for being worsted in a fight with three sailors. He is not, in any normal sense, a nice man.

One day, as Bill is herding sheep miles from anywhere, a Mexican shepherd arrives to tell Bill that unless he gets off the range, the Mexican and his fellows will kill him. When a stranger arrives that evening, Bill warns him that he really should move on, as eight Mexicans are going to come with guns. The stranger, not native to the Southwest, stays. After a small nighttime skirmish in which one Mexican is killed, a daylight gun battle occurs during which four more Mexicans are killed. So, too, is Bill. The stranger, who killed at least one of the Mexicans, notices three Mexicans limping and staggering away in the morning light. Stupefied by fatigue and fear, he moves mechanically, covering Bill with a blanket. Then he begins to leave: "He had almost reached the thicket when he stopped, smitten with alarm. A body, contorted, with one arm stiff in the air, lay in his path. Slowly and warily he moved around it, and in a moment the bushes, nodding and whispering, their leaf-faces turned toward the scene behind him, swung and swung again into stillness and the peace of the wilderness" (5:67). The luck of Richardson had abandoned Bill.[33]

The stranger is probably the most significant character in the story, for he is one of those survivors of Crane's who, like Henry Fleming in *The Red Badge*, the wounded soldier in "An Episode of War," Fred Collins in "A Mystery of Heroism," and Trescott in "The Monster," discovers a small measure of reality relating to the unknown—specifically death—and a corresponding inability to make it known. The fear

41

of death is reflected in his fear of the dead as he moves "warily around" the body of the man he has killed. His fear produces a wariness similar to that of Richardson's great fear of the blanket he could not touch. But, while Richardson has his horse to comfort and by which to be comforted, the stranger has only the unsettling indifference of the universe, which whispers in the bushes for a while, but then swings into stillness and peace.

Crane's Western stories exhibit a curious and, on the surface, rather puritanical attitude toward drink. Crane himself drank, but not excessively. Joseph Conrad tells the story of Crane's writing all day with the same glass of beer on the table. Only at the end of the day would he finish it. Crane's parents were antidrink, as strict Methodists still are. His father wrote tracts against alcohol, and his mother was an active writer and speaker for the Women's Christian Temperance Union. Crane rebelled against most of what his parents stood for, but many of his stories, particularly his Bowery and Western tales, are testaments to the dangers of drink.

The Bowery tales usually portray drink as a fact of life: life in the Bowery seems to overwhelm people, and drink inevitably offers escape from that squalor. In the Western stories, on the other hand, alcohol is used to precipitate several dangerous, or even fatal events. Scratchy Wilson "is drunk and turned loose" in "The Bride Comes to Yellow Sky." The Swede takes a drink before "fizzing like a fire-wheel" at dinner. A bloodbath occurs in "Twelve O'Clock," partly because so many people are drunk. Drunken cowboys precipitate the concern for law, order, and potential wealth in War Post in "Moonlight on the Snow." Although drink has little to do with "The Wise Men," other than that most of the story occurs in bars, in the companion piece, "The Five White Mice," drunkenness is directly responsible for nearly causing a deadly street fight. In "One Dash—Horses," the Mexicans are belligerent and murderous at least in part because they are drunk. Even Bill, in "A Man and Some Others," was in Texas, where he died, partly because of drink.

Crane's concern is not the same narrowly moral one of his parents and many other advocates of temperance; it derives rather from his interest in the self-control sometimes required for apprehending reality. Drink, as a fictional device, demonstrates people's "poor mental machinery"; their normally poor capacity for apprehension becomes even poorer under the influence of alcohol. At our most sober, we are unable to perceive much about the way things are. Drunk, we are even poorer at it, and it shows.

The two most important themes of Crane's Western stories—the vagaries of chance and the limited apprehension of reality—are related. Unlike most of us, Crane was always acutely aware that the misfortunes of chance can strike at any moment. Our ability to react appropriately is often a direct result of correct perception. In fact, Crane's most successful protagonists—those that survive: Richardson, the New York and San Francisco Kids, and Tom Larpent in the Western stories; the correspondent, the captain, and the cook in "The Open Boat," for example—do so by employing exactly the same "grace under pressure" that later became the definition of courage for Ernest Hemingway, a writer often compared to Crane. Occasionally, however, grace under pressure is not enough for survival, as is demonstrated by the deaths of Bill in "A Man and Some Others" and of the oiler in "The Open Boat." Allied to ritual in the sense that all ritual requires codes of behavior, such grace provides a response to the nihilism that comes from observing the random occurrences of this world.

Tales of Whilomville

Crane's protagonists are exiles not only from reality, but also from the group, any group. It may be exile from the fellowship of conspiracy in the Palace Hotel or, as in "The Monster" (7:7–65), from the community itself. By virtue of its setting, "The Monster" has become one of *The Whilomville Tales*, a group of stories often considered to be for children. Less violent, dichotomous, and flashy than "The Blue Hotel," "The Monster" is a domestic tragedy that, like "The Blue Hotel," reveals humanity's elemental fear of facing elemental chaos. It reveals also a three-fold purpose of community: to shield people from reality, from the howling chaos of the universe; to curb the natural, chaotic barbarity of children; and to find acceptable channels for "barbaric" expression that cannot be tethered entirely.

The longest of Crane's short stories (or the shortest of his novels), "The Monster" is not about children at all, at least if childhood is defined by chronology and not by attitude. "The Monster" is a tragic tale of oppression, and, like all tragedy, dramatizes the suffering of an ill-fated protagonist, and is bound to several rules: hamartia ("mistake" or "flaw" or simply "bad luck"), peripeteia ("reversal"), and anagnorisis ("recognition"). Fate is a kind of straightjacket that the protagonist knowingly or unknowingly dons. Slowly, the jacket tightens, and the choices become fewer and fewer. One of those choices is either wrong or simply unfortunate: the protagonist makes a mistake.

The tragic hero is Doctor Trescott, a genuinely good, rational, compassionate man, who chooses ethically but not practically. Like Antigone, Trescott confronts the conflict between private virtue and public order. He must choose between his private sense of duty and honor, which demands that he defend a man who saved his son's life, and public order, which demands that he protect the sensibilities of the community by keeping that man out of sight. Not coincidentally, that man, Henry Johnson, is black. According to J. C. Levenson, "Trescott, firmly set in the established order and prompted only by motives of which his society approved, acted to bring on himself a relentless process of exclusion and alienation."[34]

"The Monster" begins with an extended metaphor that prefigures the rest of the story. Young Jimmie Trescott is playing in his yard, a carefully manicured lawn that is consistent with the order and placidity of Whilomville. Trescott does not mow his lawn, but rather "shaves" it "as if it were a priest's chin" (7:9). Chaos confronts order when Jimmie, pretending to be a locomotive, accidentally "destroy[s] a peony" (7:9) in the flower garden. He fails to resuscitate the peony by standing it up again; its spine is crushed. A small thing, but nevertheless telling, this act shows the irrevocability of some actions, and points to later events. Just as Jimmie tries and fails to revive the peony, so his father will try later to "revive" Henry Johnson; and, just as Jimmie is banned from the well-ordered yard, so Trescott and his family will be ostracized from the community.

Jimmie then commiserates with Henry Johnson, Trescott's hired man, who is described at some length as "very handsome" and "an eminence" in the black community. More interesting is the white community's perception of him. When he dresses to go out for the evening, Henry is barely recognized by the white community used to seeing him only in relation to his work for whites. The humor seems to be directed at Henry, but the serious side of it is that the community has a distorted perception of Henry even before his accident. Crane combines an excellent Impressionistic effect and a symbol of imperfect apprehension by describing the view from a "white" barber shop window, inside of which are many men debating whether the grand figure coming down the street is Henry Johnson: "The electric shine in the street caused an effect like water to them that looked through the glass from the yellow glamour of Reifsnyder's shop. In fact, the people without resembled the inhabitants of a great aquarium that here had a square pane in it. Presently, into this frame swam the graceful form of Henry Johnson. . . . 'Ain't he a taisy?' said Reifsnyder, marvelling" (7:14).[35]

The picture of Whilomville as a clean, well-ordered place continues until, one Saturday evening, the Trescott's house catches fire. Destructive and chaotic, fires are natural enemies of communities, and the Whilomville fire companies swing quickly into action, but not before Henry Johnson rushes in to save Jimmie. Carrying Jim downstairs through flame and smoke, Henry reaches the doctor's laboratory, and falls, hitting himself on the head. A jar of acid breaks in the heat, the acid runs along the table, over the side, and drips on Johnson's "upturned face" (7:26). Trescott arrives, rushes into the house and pulls Jimmie to safety. Another man brings forth from the laboratory "a thing which he laid on the grass."

Of the many Virgilian rumors that fly about town regarding the fire, one in particular takes a long time to die: nearly everyone believes that Henry is dead. He is, of course, a hero, a dead hero, a hero because he is dead. The fire chief describes the heroics of Johnson in the newspaper, Bella "announce[s] that she had been engaged to marry Mr. Henry Johnson," and the town "turn[s] a reverent attention to the memory of this hostler" (7:30). In short, the town has decided that Henry is dead, and, having indulged in extraordinary emotions over his death, the townsfolk are not pleased to find Henry alive and even less pleased then to discover that he has "no face." Henry's loss of face is literal; the town's is figurative.

Through much quiet, private effort, however, Doctor Trescott manages to keep Johnson alive—a noble effort, but one that simultaneously becomes his hamartia, or mistake, because it violates the community's code and expectations. Trescott feels bound to do what he can for Henry; the good people of Whilomville want him out of their sight because he frightens them. Henry is harmless, but that does not matter. The mere sight of the horror, this man who bears too little outward appearance of a human being, reminds people of the essential chaos of nature, and he cannot be allowed to live in the community.

Like Job, Trescott is visited in his affliction by several "comforters" throughout the rest of the story. All give reasons for putting Johnson away. At first, Trescott tries to have it both ways by removing Johnson from sight, paying Alex Williams, a black man who lives outside town, to care for the faceless man, but when Johnson's faceless grin frightens Mrs. Williams and her children, and when the Williamses begin to be avoided by their neighbors, Alex capitulates.

Alex need not throw him out, however, for Henry escapes to town, where he frightens children and adults alike. When Henry is apprehended and jailed by the townspeople, they tell Trescott that he must "do something." The inevitable result of Henry's disfigurement, this demand produces the reversal of Trescott's fortunes, his peripeteia, and the slow exclusion of the Trescott family. Initially praised for having saved Johnson, Trescott is now damned for having done it. He refuses again to put Henry away. Anagnorisis occurs for Trescott at the story's end, when he returns home to find his wife, who had prepared for a tea party, crying. Everyone, even her best friends, has stayed away. Trescott has remained firm in his convictions. He has accepted the abuse, the minor threats, the exclusion from the community. When he discovers at the end that the community is now excluding his wife, and presumably other members of his family, he recognizes the degree of petty cruelty and injustice the community is willing to inflict on those who insist on reminding them of the horror of nature: "As he sat holding her head on his shoulder, Trescott found himself trying to count the cups. There were fifteen of them" (7:65). Just as many of Crane's other protagonists gain a tiny glimpse of reality by observing the minutiae of nature—tree bark, leaves, grass, and the like—Trescott gains his by seeing the minutiae of civilization: teacups.

"The Monster" is one of Crane's richest stories, containing a great range of significance. Crane not only exposes the intolerance of small-town life, but also explores the failure of democracy in America to grant equality. Henry is a black man destroyed by fire and ignorance just as thoroughly as the picture on the wall of the Trescott home is destroyed: "In the hall a lick of flame had found the cord that supported 'Signing the Declaration' " (7:21). Of the three guarantees provided by the Declaration of Independence—"life, liberty, and the pursuit of happiness"—the fire and Whilomville destroy the latter two for Henry. Moreover, Crane explores another aspect of his belief that "conceit is the very engine of life": a faceless, witless man turns an "unwinking eye" to people who see reflected in it themselves, and the vanity and essentially chaotic nature of human life and endeavor. We are made monsters by refusing to see that chaos is all around us and we would probably be monsters if we did not deny it. Henry Johnson is a mild reminder. Should we have but the slightest intimation of reality, as Emily Dickinson said, the calmest of us would be lunatics. Trescott does all anyone can do, and that is ultimately a losing battle. By being ethical in the face of overwhelming odds, Trescott shows us how to live at the same time he shows us, paradoxically, Crane's nihilistic vision.[36]

Not everyone agrees that the story is nihilistic. Robert A. Morace, for example, claims that real choices are within reach, and that "the point is that the town *can* choose to stop the game [of excluding the Trescotts] but does not."[37] Towns, however, cannot make ethical choices; only individuals can. Ethical choices require courage, and communities too easily become mobs, and "the mob," says Crane, "has no courage." "The Monster" reinforces Crane's belief that communities exist, in part, to inhibit ethical choice.[38] When a man like Trescott insists on making such a choice, he is made to suffer for it.

One should neither over- nor under-emphasize the fact that Johnson is a black man. As were many blacks in turn-of-the-century America, Johnson is tolerated by white society only because he "behaves himself " and "knows his place"; he is a small town version of Conrad's harlequin in *The Heart of Darkness*. Crane was hardly a civil-rights activist. A story called "The Knife" (7:184–94), for example, which Crane himself calls "an effete joke," hangs on the old stereotype regarding blacks and watermelons.[39] The power of Crane's art, the accuracy and profundity of his portrayal in "The Monster," reveals truths not socially accepted for almost another hundred years. The story is, indeed, an excoriation of social conditions for blacks, but more important (and it must indeed be important to be more important), it is an excoriation of all communities, all societies, in all places and all times.

Moreover, that Johnson is faceless is more important than that he is black. Essentially harmless, Johnson is more "natural" than the artificial villagers. When this faceless man is allowed to walk among the good citizens of Whilomville, Henry reminds them of what they might be were the thin veneer of civilization stripped away, if acid ate the face of Whilomville, if their reason were suddenly destroyed, if community fell apart and they had to face the unwinking eye of nature alone. The community must remove Henry at any cost. It is this that Trescott sees when he tries to count the teacups.

There is more. So rich is this story that it invites explanations from all ranges of traditional criticism of Crane's work. As Morace says, critics have noted "biblical, literary, and biographical sources. . . . It has been read as Naturalism, Existentialism, social protest, Christian allegory, and has been twice subjected to Freudian interpretation."[40] Joseph Conrad, perhaps the closest friend Crane had in his adult life and whose own story of "the horror" would become a classic, was haunted by "The Monster."[41] William Dean Howells thought it "the greatest story ever written by an American."[42] More business-minded contemporaries, however, recognized the nihilism at the center of the story and shrank from publishing it. Paul Revere Reynolds, Crane's American agent, heard from one editor who rejected the story by saying, "we couldn't publish that thing with half the expectant mothers in America on our subscription list!"[43]

"The Monster" also provides examples of several of the themes and symbols that appear periodically throughout Crane's fiction. One of these is the stove. Stoves appear three times in "The Monster," always as symbols of order, especially of a kind of order that symbolizes safety for the group, in this case, a family. The stove's first appearance occurs when the faceless Henry appears in Alex Williams's home, and six of his children make "a simultaneous plunge for a position behind the stove" (7:35). Later, when Alex goes cautiously to check Henry's room, Mrs. Williams "stood in front of the stove, and her arms were spread out in the natural movement to protect all her sleeping ducklings" (7:44). A stove makes a final appearance, this time ironically, in the last lines of the story, near the teacups: "A low table had been drawn close to the stove, . . . [the table] was burdened with many small cups . . ." (7:64). In the Williams home, the stove offers unnecessary protection from the harmless Johnson; in Trescott's, it offers no protection from the angered community.

Crane's tragedies, then, range from the heroic in "The Blue Hotel" to the nihilistic in "The Monster." We come away from "The Blue Hotel" with a belief that while truth-telling has a price and is ultimately unsustainable, truth does exist. From "The Monster" we take a sense of futility, a black despair deriving from a sense of the inevitable triumph of wrong over right, of community over individual, of blindness over sight.

Most tragedies, for all their temporary despair, right things in the end, and most tragedies, therefore, belong to a genre of hope. At the end of "The Monster," however, the only one who learns anything remains powerless to continue the good fight. A doctor cannot earn a living in a town from which he is ostracized. "The Monster" is an ironic tragedy. Great short stories rarely provide definitive answers, but they do raise very important questions.

After "The Monster," Crane continued with less ambitious stories of Whilomville. Around this time, too, he knew he was fatally ill and almost fatally in debt. The fever he had contracted in Cuba weakened him and aggravated the tuberculosis that was to kill him. Under these shadows, he wrote most of the remaining "Whilomville Stories." "Whilomville" has been seen as a kind of utopia, a fictional American small town of a type in which anyone would wish to have grown up. Levenson, for example, sees Whilomville as Crane's "town of Once-upon-a-time, the ideal American small town of memory and imagination."[44] And if Crane were given to nostalgia, there might be some truth to that interpretation. Whilomville seems clearly to have been modeled on Port Jervis, New York, where Crane's brother William lived and where Crane himself lived from the ages of seven to twelve,[45] but the stories are not simple nostalgic tales, not about "once-upon-a-time." Although "whilom" means "once-upon-a-time," the stories partake of the tragic sense of a remote and indefinite past, and because the events they depict belong to the past, they cannot be undone. The stories convey the feeling that growing up in America, or perhaps anywhere, is tragic.

Most of the stories are about children (with the exception of Doctor Trescott and a very few others, there are no grown-ups in Whilomville), but only nominally so. The children in Crane's Whilomville exhibit all the foibles and fears, evil and good, barbarism and civilization that their elders exhibit more subtly. Eric Solomon makes an excellent case for seeing these tales as parodies of "The boyhood volumes written by [Crane's] contemporaries" George W. Peck, Thomas Bailey Aldrich, Charles Dudley Warner, Booth Tarkington, and even William Dean Howells.[46] Thomas Gullason sees the Whilomville tales as a "novel," for "each episode contributes to the emerging significance."[47] Gullason also remarks, and rightly, that while the tales are *about* children, they are *for* adults.[48] Holton sees the Whilomville tales more darkly, and I think rightly, as "how the Whilomville of the child shapes the apprehension of the man"[49] and "how distortions of apprehension are engendered and enforced by a child's relationship with his peers and with his parents."[50]

While adult readers may see in these stories events of their own childhoods, and see again how "the child is father of the man" or mother of the woman, the Whilomville tales are also about the small town as insulation from chaos. The stories gain further artistic and philosophical significance, moreover, because Crane includes an ironic turn of the screw. In these stories, children are seen as humorously barbaric and uncivilized. Because they are threats to civilization, the children are upbraided constantly by adults, whose job it is to civilize the children. The adults, however, are no more civilized than the children, and their efforts are made in the name of the same barbaric qualities, although more hidden and therefore insidious, as those embodied in the children. All the egotism of the children, their naked self-centeredness, ambition, and lawlessness become enlarged and paradoxically hidden in adults who use the "town" as a mask for these qualities.

"His New Mittens," a tale of children in Whilomville, was originally published in *McClure's Magazine* in November 1898 and became part of *The Monster and Other Stories* published by Harper in 1899. It was the only tale of childhood in that volume. Thirteen other stories were published between August 1899 and August 1900 (Crane died in June) in *Harper's New Monthly Magazine*. Each of these 14 stories, 13 of them collected in *Tales of Whilomville*, presents some aspects of chaos, usually represented by the children; and of egotism, always represented by the children, but often by adults as well.

Horace Glenn, the little protagonist of "His New Mittens," is caught between the demands of two groups: his youthful companions and his family. Enjoined by his mother not to ruin his new mittens by getting them wet, Horace tries to avoid joining a snowball fight after school, but fails. He is caught by his mother, and suffers the humiliation of being dragged home by the ear.

Much of the story turns on the motif of food. Food is used to corrupt the natural tendency of children to rebel, to move outside the family and the community, and, perhaps, even to confront chaos. His humiliation at his mother's perceived injustices is such that he resolves to make her pay dearly by refusing to eat. Alone in the kitchen, Horace is sorely tempted to eat, but manages "not to sell his vengeance for bread, cold ham, and a pickle. . . . She must pay the inexorable penalty" (7:88–89). He runs away into a snowstorm, heading first for a woodshed and then for the butcher shop, which displays "rows of glowing pigs," "huge pieces of red beef," and "clumps of attenuated turkeys" (7:92). Stickney, the butcher, sees him, understands, and takes Horace home. Mother and child embrace in a tearful reunion. Aunt Martha offers the butcher—food: " 'Won't you have a glass of our root-beer, Mr. Stickney? We make it ourselves' " (7:93). In effect, food turns the tables on Horace. Wanting to punish his mother for making him conform to adult rules, he suffers relentlessly, thinking more about food, the sum and substance of motherly love in this story, than about escape. Horace cannot escape; he cannot even learn anything about escaping from Whilomville. Chaos is too frightening and communal ties too strong to admit of learning.

"The Angel-Child" (7:129–37), the first story in the volume, is the old story of the city mouse and country mouse, but also contains a number of ironic twists. The first is that the city mouse, a thoroughly spoiled little girl named Cora, never gets her comeuppance. Indeed, before her imperious actions all others remain impotent. The story opens with a description of a family visit to the Trescotts, one of Whilomville's first families, by Cora's parents and Cora, a child of whom the narrator says, "perhaps it would be better to say that they had one CHILD" (7:129). Jimmie Trescott and the neighborhood children quickly become her slaves: "They at first feared, then admired, then embraced. . . . All day long her voice could be heard directing, drilling, and compelling those free-born children, and . . . they fought for records of loyal obedience" (7:130).

On Cora's birthday, her father unthinkingly gives her five dollars. She first buys the other children so much ice cream and candy that they nearly become ill. She next takes everyone to a barber, an incompetent barber. Cora is not alone in having carefully coiffured hair. The other girls, and even some of the boys, have long, beautifully curled locks. In an extended parody, Crane uses mock-epic language to describe the hair-cutting in a manner reminiscent of Pope's in *The Rape of the Lock*: "The queen herself [Cora] took the chair . . . To the floor there fell proud ringlets blazing even there in their humiliation with a full fine bronze light" (7:133).ꞌ When they leave, the children leave their beautiful hair behind.

In his fiction, Crane never got over his century's notion that women were somehow more "civilized," "refined," and delicate than men. It was generally assumed by nineteenth-century Americans that women were "society"—that segment of the social organism that determines mores and codes of behavior—and that by shrieking, swooning, and reacting (they seldom acted) in other ways we may now consider ridiculous, women could enforce the agreed-upon code of "civilized" behavior. Nevertheless, such is the power of society that Crane's portrayal is more a nasty exaggeration and a parody of manners than a lie:

> "Oh, mamma," shrieked little Cora, "see how fine I am! I've had my hair cut! Isn't it splendid! And Jimmie too."
> The wretched mother took one sight, emitted one yell and fell into a chair. . . . (7:134)

The reaction is repeated all over town as parents see their children's hair. Naturally, the visit of Mrs. Trescott's cousin and his family is cut short. Cora's mother blames her husband for giving the money to the child: "he was the guilty one—he!"

In one sense, "The Angel-Child" appears to be a slight tale. Even on the level of the relationship between men and women—the women carry on and the men try to stay out of the way—it seldom goes beyond stock responses. Embedded in the primary story, however, is another one that hints at the communal oppression of any who do not belong, who upset the fragile order of Whilomville, who remind the citizens of the chaos that is evident in many of Crane's other stories. The barber, William Neeltje, becomes, like Henry Johnson in "The Monster," a pariah. In this context, although Neeltje is not the major figure in the story, he is more significant than he initially seems to be. While the good native citizen who sells the children too much ice cream and candy is described in only two sentences, Neeltje, the barber, is a foreigner, and is described in detail and scrutinized by the narrator:

> He was new to the town. He had come and opened a dusty little shop on dusty Bridge Street hill and although the neighborhood knew from the courier winds that his diet was mainly cabbages, they were satisfied with that meagre data. Of course, Reifsnyder came to investigate him for the local Barbers' Union, but he found in him only sweetness and light, with a willingness to charge anything at all for a shave or a hair-cut. In fact the advent of Neeltje would have made barely a ripple upon the placid bosom of Whilomville if it were not that his name was Neeltje. (7:132)

There follows, in a paragraph nearly twice as long as the one quoted here, a description of the townmen's unsuccessful attempts to learn to pronounce his name. On one level the business of Neeltje's name is a bad ethnic joke, which is one way the town finds to deal with those who are different; on another, it is Crane's way of showing, humorously, the attempts of an organism to circumscribe a foreign agent introduced into its body.

Like Henry Johnson, Neeltje becomes the object of potential terrorism. It is not only that he disturbs the complaisant calm of Whilomville by shearing the children; it is also that by his very existence, he disturbs that calm. Among the shorn children were the Margate twins, and the Margates are not pleased, especially the older women, who demand that Eldridge Margate, the grandfather and patriarch of the family, excise the foreign element: "The feminine Margates stormed his position as individuals, in pairs, in teams and en masse. . . . He must destroy the utter Neeltje" (7:136). Eldridge Margate, himself, thinks better of it. Talking with Trescott, Margate says "I might go and burn his shop over his head but that won't bring no hair back onto the kids" (7:137). And Trescott, who in "The Monster" faces a similar situation, "perceived that the old man wore his head above his shoulders. . . ." Although nothing comes of the women's demands because the men still can see Neeltje as a joke (he may be a foreigner, but he is not faceless), the same sense of communal outrage that threatens to destroy Trescott in "The Monster" is vented in the howling madness of the Margates, an outrage which, one suspects, has been echoed in other households throughout Whilomville.

"The Stove" (7:195–206) is the only other story about the spoiled and willful angel-child. A stiff ritual of adult life, the tea party, is ruined by children imitating the rituals of adults. Visiting the Trescotts during Christmas, little Cora and her parents bring a stove—small but functional—because it "pleases" Cora. While the tea party is in full swing upstairs, Cora and her slave Jimmie Trescott are cooking turnips in the cellar. The smell of burnt turnips rises to the tea party, and brings it to an end.

The point of the story seems to be not only the absurdity of communal rituals (as opposed to individual rituals) that "make life even more uncomfortable," but also how the rituals of women make life uncomfortable for men. Jimmie is ordered here and there, and is compromised by little Cora. In the parallel adult world upstairs, Doctor Trescott and Willis, Cora's father, flee "to the lengths of their tethers" (7:198). The power of feminine rituals is reinforced by the ending. Trescott and Willis discover the source of the smell, and Trescott demands that Willis spank his child: "Spank her, confound you, man! She needs it. Here's your chance" (7:205). Willis spanks Cora, but the mother soon arrives, takes "her child to her bosom," and looks "bitterly, scornfully, at the cowering father and husband" (7:206). Willis, "for his part, at once looked reproachfully at Trescott as if to say: 'There! You see?' "

Holton speculates on Crane's rather clear belittlement of women in the Whilomville stories, and in a footnote places Crane's fictional women among the "dark ladies" of American fiction.[51] In "Shame," "one of the more complex and profound of the stories," according to Holton,[52] Jimmie Trescott is caught between two groups of women—adults and children—as was the protagonist of "His New Mittens." The adults expect him to appear at a picnic. The children, "especially . . . some of those damnable little girls," he knows, will deride him if he appears carrying his lunch in a pail, the only receptacle available to him. He goes because he is expected to, and he is derided as he expected to be. The situation is saved, however, when a "beautiful lady" sits by him: "His face was glorified; he had forgotten all about the pail; he was absorbed in communion with this beautiful lady" (7:170).

This theme of damned-if-he-does and damned-if-he-doesn't is repeated at the end. Returning home after seeing the lady to her door, Jimmie realizes he has not eaten his sandwich. He knows that the cook will be angry and hurt if she discovers he has not eaten it. He runs to the barn and hides the sandwich under some blankets. The cook is satisfied to see the empty pail. The hostler and handyman, Peter Washington, however, is angry to find a fish sandwich under his blankets. Rightly, he blames Jimmie.

"Shame" demonstrates one of the fantasies available to the children of Whilomville. Unable to bear the strictures of the group, Jimmie is offered a way out in the form of an older woman. Given Crane's view of women—even considering that, in his life, he loved only "older" women—the reality will never live up to the fantasy. Once again, a true perception of reality is deliberately diverted by the community into fantasy.

"Lynx-Hunting" (7:138–43) is a curious tale. The story is the third and last time Crane would include Henry Fleming into his fiction. Fleming is a grown man, and the period is sometime after the Civil War but before his death in "The Veteran." Willie Dalzel, who has a shotgun, takes Jimmie Trescott and another boy into the woods to hunt a lynx, an animal they have never seen before, and are not likely to see now. After shooting a couple of birds, Willie and the other boy give the gun to Trescott. Jimmie promptly aims at a chipmunk and promptly misses it, hitting, however, a cow, which then bellows across the field toward home. The boys are frightened. They are even more frightened when a Swede, Fleming's hired hand, catches them. Facing Fleming, the boys grovel, whine, and blame each other until Fleming asks who shot the cow. When Jimmie confesses that he thought the cow was a lynx, Fleming and the Swede fall to the ground laughing and the story ends. The criminal act that had forced young Henry Fleming, in *The Red Badge of Courage*, to lie to his fellow soldiers and to cause him excruciating pain, is here transferred to a little boy. That the result is laughter seems to absolve not only Jimmie Trescott, but Henry Fleming as well.

"The Carriage-Lamps" (7:173–83), like "Lynx-Hunting," is another story of boyish crimes left unpunished. Both stories end with grown-up laughter. When Doctor Trescott discovers from his hired man, Peter Washington, that Jimmie has acquired a small revolver through barter, he takes it away from the boy. In the course of throwing small stones at the hostler for telling on him, Jimmie breaks the glass on a carriage-lamp. Confined to the house to await his punishment, Jimmie talks through an open window to Willie Dalzel, who promises to "rescue" him from his "excwable enemies and their vile plots" (7:182). As Willie returns to the window with several other boys to rescue Jim, Doctor Trescott enters the room. Comprehending, Trescott sits away from the window and listens to the high-flown adventure-novel language of the boys in the midst of their rescue. As usual, Jimmie is caught between two worlds. The boys finally are frightened away, but Jimmie goes unpunished, for his father is laughing too much to think of punishment.

Once again Doctor Trescott is seen as a reasonable man, although he initially gets caught up in the character assassination of Willie Dalzel rather than admit lawlessness in one of his own blood: " 'I should think that those Dalzel people would hire somebody to bring up their child for them,' said the doctor. 'They don't seem to know how to do it themselves' " (7:177). The humor of the situation at the end reveals Trescott's natural good sense. He knows that Willie is not the culprit. Once again, Trescott finds himself at odds with accepted notions of society, this time expressed by Peter Washington, having discovered Jimmie unpunished, in words meaning much the same as those Trescott himself used to damn Willie's parents: "Dede yer white folks act like they think er boy's made er glass. No trouncin'!" (7:182).

"The Lover and the Tell-Tale" (7:144–49), and "Showin' Off" (7:150–57) demonstrate again the power of communal standards over individual behavior. In both stories the group wins. In "The Lover," Jimmie Trescott is caught in a heinous crime—writing to a girl, little Cora of "The Angel-Child"—by the "tell-tale" Rose Goldege. There follows baiting "beyond the borders of sanity," fights, and, as a result, the teacher's strictures and demands that Jimmie stay after school. The story ends with Rose Goldege, a miniature bastion of Whilomville's morality, in an ecstacy of superiority at having exposed Jimmie's sins: "When he took his seat he saw gloating upon him the satanic black eyes of the little Goldege girl" (7:149).

"Showin' Off" differs slightly from "The Lover" in that the punishment is completely self-imposed. Jimmie Trescott, "accompanied by one of his retainers," follows home that week's object of his adoration and tries to impress her in various ways. The girl may or may not be impressed, but his attempts to impress her threaten to be overshadowed when another boy, Horace, comes by on his velocipede, an early bicycle. Jimmie and Horace argue over who can ride better and faster. Jimmie brags that he can ride it faster than Horace. Horace responds by daring Jimmie to ride it down a small ravine at the bottom of which are ashes and empty cans. Jimmie accepts. Horace remembers that he does not allow anyone else to ride his velocipede. Everyone then dares Horace to do it, and he does, unintentionally. Horace is hurt, and Jimmie and the other boy run home. For once, Jimmie Trescott does not have to pay the price for "showing off." In both stories, however—the one an exhibition of heredity or environment, the other of instinct or tribalism—someone must pay. In this instance, Horace does. One can almost hear the boy cry out the title of his famous namesake's poem, "Ave atque vale," as he hurls down the bank.

"Making an Orator" (7:158–63) is about another poem, Tennyson's "The Charge of the Light Brigade" (1855), which glorifies the fatal and stupid charge of British cavalry through two ranks of cannon during the Crimean War. Jimmie Trescott appears again, and again in misery. He must recite "The Charge of the Light Brigade" on whatever Friday his turn comes, and, although "he learned all the verses," he is deathly afraid of speaking before the class. After pretending to be ill for two Fridays, "on the third Friday, Jimmie was dropped at the door of the school" (7:159). His fear keeps him from remembering the lines. The teacher keeps him after school, telling him that he must recite the poem next Friday.

On one level it is a humorous story made all the more humorous for reminding the adult reader of a childhood spent in fear of recitation. It is also a bitter attack on schools for imposing such cruelty on children. Recitation, says the narrator, "operated mainly to antagonize many children permanently against arising to speak their thoughts to fellow-creatures" (7:159). Moreover, "Jimmie of course did not know that there had been laid for him the foundation of a finished incapacity for public speaking which would be his until he died" (7:163). On another level, the significance of the poem comes to bear. One suspects that, in Crane's ironic view, there is little difference in motive between forcing children to recite poetry and forcing young men to ride to their deaths in war. In "Making an Orator," Crane dramatizes society's amazing power to make people do incomprehensible things. Charging to certain death is incomprehensible; reciting a poem, the words of which remain incomprehensible to the speaker, is equally incomprehensible. Jimmie recites "half a league, half a league, half a league onward," but has no idea of the distance of a league: "If . . . somebody had told him that he was half a league from home he might have been frightened that half a league was fifty miles" (7:159). Only Crane's editorializing keeps this from being an excellent story. The narrator, for example, does not need to tell the reader that recitation operates "mainly to antagonize many children permanently against arising to speak their thoughts to fellow-creatures" (7:159).

Despite its faults, the story shows Crane's consistent use of a method he turns to in some of his best work: universalizing a situation by creating a metaphor from the particular. "The Charge of the Light Brigade," employed in this manner, is an apt, even brutal metaphor for universalizing and making significant society's murder of a boy's inclinations toward public speaking, as well as society's inclination toward murdering boys.

"The Trial, Execution, and Burial of Homer Phelps" (7:207–15) is a chilling tale of initiation into community, the high price for which is a mock-death, a mock-death that becomes real death in "The Upturned Face" Crane was to write a few weeks later. It is also reminiscent of Henry Johnson's "death" in "The Monster." Like all the Whilomville stories, "The Trial" is a "children's story" on the surface. Boys are playing in the winter woods. One boy fails to give the password upon entering the camp. The others decide that this boy, Homer Phelps, must be tried for his crime. It is a foregone conclusion that he will then be executed and buried. Homer demurs, but after Jimmie Trescott shows him how to undergo the ritual trial and execution, Homer agrees to be buried.

The story is about initiation into the same group that forms, or rather will form when its members grow up, the community of Whilomville. The price is high: utter conformity and ritual death. The ritualized death is metaphorical, and symbolizes the death of individuality. Moreover, the group never fully accepts Homer. Most of us remember the perpetual outsider in the little gangs of our youth: usually someone who is "different" in some way, and, by virtue of that difference, is never quite accepted. Homer Phelps appears to be that boy in Whilomville. Not only is he "killed" in this story, but later, in "The City Urchin and the Chaste Villagers" (7:227–34), he is again selected to play the part of victim, the "cabin boy" who remains friendless and despised throughout most of the reenactment of a "pirate novel": "Willie Dalzel developed a scheme by which some small lad would play cabin-boy during this period of misfortune and abuse and then when the cabin-boy came to the part where he slew all his enemies and reached his zenith that he, Willie Dalzel, should take the part. . . . Then Willie Dalzel insisted that Homer Phelps should be the cabin-boy" (7:230).

If "The Trial" is about a boy who wants to be accepted into the already-established group, "The Fight" (7:216–26) is about a boy from the "outside" (a kind of "foreigner" like Neeltje) who threatens to overthrow the established order. Johnnie Hedge, whose surname places him on the periphery of the territory, is a new boy in town. When Willie and his gang first see Hedge, "They looked him over; he looked them over. They might have been savages observing the first white man or white men observing the first savage" (7:217). After asking "What's your name?" and "Where'd you live b'fore?" Willie says, "I kin lick you." Hedge answers, "I know you kin." Next in line to fight is Jimmie, and a stalemate occurs. Later, on Johnnie's first day at school, the children jeer at him, make fun in various ways, and generally make him feel miserable. Cornered in the schoolyard, Hedge introduces the use of fists from his native New Jersey, and whips everyone, including the boys' leader, Willie Dalzel.

"The City Urchin and the Chaste Villagers" continues the story begun in "The Fight." The "little community" cannot succumb "to the boy who could whip all others," for he is an outsider; neither can it turn to Willie, for he "had run away" (7:227). While Hedge "maintain[s] a curious timid reserve. . . ," perhaps recognizing his chief adversary, the other boys hoot and whistle, and otherwise deride Willie Dalzel from the "sanctity of their own yards." The child-community is threatened: because of his prowess, Johnnie Hedge has upset the entire social order, and "every boy" is "anxious that Johnnie's position should soon be established." That is, order must be restored from this social chaos.

Having read dime novels about pirate ships and cabin boys who suffer torment and disgrace, only to become swashbuckling captains, Willie decides to reassert his leadership by reenacting such a novel. His leadership is challenged when none of his former subordinates will play the role of despised cabin-boy. After Homer Phelps refuses, Johnnie Hedge's little brother accepts the role: "When he was invited to become the cabin-boy he accepted joyfully thinking that it was his initiation into the tribe. Then they proceeded . . . to punch him with a realism that was not altogether painless" (7:230). After a fracas, Johnnie's mother grabs him and boxes his ears, and the narrator concludes, "the war for supremacy was over and the question was never again disputed. The supreme power was Mrs. Hedge" (7:234). Although the boys do not dispute again, the notion remains that power is essentially physical, thus undermining the notion of Whilomville as a rural utopia. Power resides with the strongest, as it does in the most primitive and savage tribes.

The final Whilomville story, "A Little Pilgrim" (7:235–39), collects from the other stories all the meanness, the tribalism, the communal degradation of individuality, and the brainwashing cruelty of society, and casts a religious light on them. The particular religion is irrelevant. The Trescotts are "consistently undenominational" and the two churches represented are inoffensively Protestant: the Presbyterian and the "Big Progressive." Jimmie Trescott normally attends the Presbyterian Sunday school, but when the Sunday School Superintendent gives an impassioned speech asking that the children forego buying a Christmas tree in favor of sending money to the victims of an earthquake, the children are caught in the emotion of the moment, and vote to relieve the suffering of the victims. Almost immediately, Jimmie decides that the other Sunday school would be more to his liking. So, he endures the trials of a new Sunday school, only to find that, not to be outdone by the Presbyterians, the Big Progressive church also will forego a Christmas tree.

"A Little Pilgrim"[53] would be a slight story indeed if it were not that several descriptions of Sunday school raise the level of meaning several notches, and the story moves from a depiction of child-like discomfort to communal repression, and perhaps contains a metaphor for the oppression humanity forces on itself. The children are quoted the Bible's "trust ye not in lying words," but to trust "the temple of the Lord"—that is, the church. The Sunday school teacher and the superintendent and the church board make themselves feel very good by depriving the children of their Christmas tree. The story of Daniel in the lion's den, which, metaphorically, is where the children are, means nothing more to the children than that Daniel was "in the wrong place" (children seem to understand the power of chance), but to the adult "angels," it means that "we should be very good." The children are forced to give up something they hold very dear for people they neither know nor have ever seen. The church elders sacrifice their children on the altar of their own emotional slither. Just as individuals are powerless against the community, so reason is impotent before the juggernaut of communal emotion.[54] Finally, the narrator mentions a picture on the wall behind the superintendent's chair called the "Martyrdom of St. Stephen." One wonders whether the young Stephen Crane had had the experience depicted in this story.

Tales of War

Given the swift and soaring success of *The Red Badge of Courage*, it is hardly surprising that Crane wrote many short stories about three wars, one he never saw and two that he did see: the American Civil War (1861–65), the Greco-Turkish War of 1897, and the Spanish-American War of 1898. Seventeen of these stories appeared during his lifetime in two volumes: *The Little Regiment* and *Wounds in the Rain*. There are others: "An Episode of War," written too late to appear in *The Little Regiment;* four stories collected in the *Works* as *Spitzbergen Tales;*[55] and several scattered pieces.

Although Crane eventually returned to the subject of war, as a way to the heart of "the real thing," the early success of *The Red Badge of Courage* left him in a peculiar artistic dilemma. On one hand, the novel was responsible for making Crane one of America's first literary "stars." On the other, it violated his own youthful belief, one espoused by his literary mentors Howells and Garland, that the truth—to the extent that it could be seen and reported—had to be experienced first-hand. *The Red Badge* described a war that had ended more than six years before Crane was born. Nor had Crane even seen a war, let alone experienced a battle, before he wrote the novel that made him famous in 1895.

He was reluctant to follow the success of *The Red Badge* with other war stories for another reason: he believed, as he said, that "I have used myself up on the accursed *Red Badge*." In spite of the "damned 'Red Badge,'" Crane agreed to write more war stories because of the hounding of his publisher, McClure, and a ubiquitous need for money.[56] His efforts resulted in *The Little Regiment*, published late in 1896. Crane called *The Little Regiment* a novelette,[57] perhaps in the same way that we think of Hemingway's *In Our Time* and Joyce's *Dubliners* as "novelettes" of closely linked short stories. Although the stories employ many of the same methods and themes as *The Red Badge*, it is important to note that there are marked exceptions, and that some of the themes are different from those of the war novel.

The Little Regiment comprises six stories: "The Little Regiment"

(6:3–21), "Three Miraculous Soldiers" (6:22–47), "A Mystery of Heroism" (6:48–56), "An Indiana Campaign" (6:57–66), "A Grey Sleeve" (6:67–81), and "The Veteran" (6:82–86). The typical hero of these stories is the naive man, similar to the "little man" of the Sullivan County tales: unaware of his naiveté, he misinterprets events. The recurrent motif is the contrast between the hero's deluded sense of order and the chaos of the universe, which is represented by the vast indifference of war. Unlike *The Red Badge* and Crane's later war stories, those in *The Little Regiment* come closest to portraying the protagonists not as isolated individuals, but as undifferentiated naturalistic types. Whereas Henry Fleming, the youthful protagonist of *The Red Badge*, spends most of the novel separating himself from the group, the protagonists of *The Little Regiment* are identified not as individuals but as members of a group. Like the Bowery sketches, these stories compose Crane's foray into naturalism: the protagonists are not individualized human beings, but representatives of "humanity." Because Crane's talent and vision were not amenable to naturalistic methods, the results in *The Little Regiment* are sometimes disappointing.

The title story of the volume—which, like *The Red Badge*, may have been based on a real battle and thus gained authority in Crane's mind as "realism,"[58]—is disappointing. Initially, the story seems mistitled: it is not about a regiment but rather about two brothers in a regiment, Dan and Billie. The first section describes the regiment as it prepares for battle, but then the story focuses on the two brothers, who are nearly always arguing. They had argued when they had enlisted; they argue when they are fighting others; they clearly despise each other, or so it seems to everyone in the regiment. Advancing into battle, Billie recognizes his utter insignificance, and recognizes as well a fit punishment for Dan: Billie will ignore him. If the universe can ignore Billie, and Billie is offended, then Billie can offend Dan by ignoring him.

Part 2 shows the negative effects of Billie's indifference to Dan, but when Billie turns up missing, Dan becomes genuinely concerned. At the end, Billie returns, wounded: "The man with a bandage . . . moved forward, always shaking hands and explaining. At times his glance wandered to Dan, who sat with his eyes riveted. . . . Finally, [Billie] said: 'Hello, Dan.' " Dan responds: " 'Hello, Billie' " (6:21). In short, they need each other. The difference between the private needs of Dan and Billie and the public need of the men for the regiment is that Dan and Billie express the need through irony, by conveying to each other the opposite of what they feel. The men of the regiment, however, express their need openly: "Of their own corps they spoke with a deep veneration, an idolatry, a supreme confidence . . ." (6:11). Finally, the story presents a variation on the theme of the egotism necessary for living. Alone on this space-lost bulb, men attach themselves to something outside themselves in order to create order and a sense of importance. Billie and Dan believe that their own importance is diminished by the other until they find something that diminishes their importance even more. At that point, they realize what they had always known instinctively: that the other's existence increases their own importance, just as the existence of the regiment surpasses in importance the lives of its individual members. As the story's main theme is one of community, "The Little Regiment" is not misnamed after all.

Another story depicting this parallel between private attachments and public is "A Grey Sleeve," which tells a love story about a Union officer and a Confederate woman. Crane describes it as "not in any sense a good story" and its protagonists as "a pair of idiots."[59] He is not far wrong. One may view the story as a parody of high-flown Romantic war fiction. The "young captain" has a "reddish, bronze complexion," "yellow hair," and a "bright saber held threateningly." He is dashing and brave. The "young girl" tries to keep Union soldiers from searching her house by holding a pistol on them, all the while imploring them "Please, don't go up there" (6:73). Her resolve weakens and she sinks "down upon the step," weeping in "agony and with convulsive tremors" (6:74). Confronted with this weeping puddle, the young and gallant captain is undone: "Ah, don't cry like that." Remembering to become gallant again, he protects the girl from his men: "You touch that girl and I'll split your skull" (6:75). Discovering the girl's aged father and wounded brother, both Confederates, the Union officer ignores the rules of war by ordering his men to ride off gallantly, as if no one had been in the house. As he leaves he engages in a banal bit of banter with the girl. She wants to see him again. His hopes rise. Then she doesn't. His hopes fall. Then she does. His hopes rise. Then she says . . . and the story ends, far too late to save it from silliness.

"Three Miraculous Soldiers" is another story of men and women and war. A Confederate girl hides three Confederate soldiers in her barn and helps them to escape from Union soldiers. Like the Swede of "The Blue Hotel," this young Southern belle has been reading too much fiction: "Heroines, she knew, conducted these matters with infinite precision and despatch. They severed the hero's bonds, cried a dramatic sentence, and stood between him and his enemies until he

63

had run far enough away." Like the Swede, she confronts the disparity between illusion and reality. Unlike the Swede, she confronts them with a clear, almost undeluded eye throughout the story. Realizing that if she stood between the escaping soldiers and the Union soldiers, "those grim troops in blue would not pause. They would run around her, make a circuit. One by one she saw the gorgeous contrivances and expedients of fiction fall before the plain, homely difficulties of this situation" (6:33).

And indeed there are many homely difficulties. During a small skirmish in the orchard, one of the Union soldiers is wounded, and all three Southerners escape. The girl, having watched all this through a knothole in the barn wall, becomes concerned for the Union soldier. So far, not a bad story. It ends, however, with two Union officers moralizing on the Rebel girl's concern for the soldier in blue.

> "Queer," said a young officer. "Girl very clearly worst kind of rebel and yet she falls to weeping and wailing like mad over one of her enemies. . . ."
> The sharp lieutenant shrugged his shoulders. After reflection he shrugged his shoulders again. He said: "War changes many things, but it doesn't change everything, thank God." (6:47)

Conversations between Crane's men and women are almost invariably a muddle of sighs, furtive glances, blushes, and stutterings. Except when his parody is conscious and artful, as in "The Bride" and "The Pace of Youth," Crane seems more nervous, heavy-handed, and unsure of himself than the characters he describes. Even this brave and intelligent Confederate girl, who comes to realize the difference between illusion and reality, and who, like Crane's most significant heroes—Henry Fleming, the Swede, the Correspondent, Judge Trescott, and Peza—attempts as hard as they to apprehend, to understand the significance of things, is finally a stereotype. Unlike the others—all males—she fails to be redeemed from that stereotype.

Although the male world of soldiering often becomes sentimentalized, as in "The Little Regiment," at least it does not often become insipid, unlike Crane's romances. Several all-male, or nearly all-male stories, contain redeeming features. Two stories, "A Mystery of Heroism" (6:48–56) and "An Indiana Campaign" (6:57–66), turn on a plot Crane used repeatedly in the *Sullivan County Sketches*: the necessity to do something dangerous (or something perceived as dangerous) in or-

der to save face. In "A Mystery of Heroism" the "necessity" is created
by a dare much like that of the children in "Showin' Off." The difference between these confrontations and those in the earlier stories is
that Crane now embarks on a kind of fiction in which the stakes are
higher. In most of the earlier *Sullivan County Sketches*, the worst that
can happen may be to suffer derision from one's fellows, a bruised ego,
or a sore shoulder. With "A Mystery of Heroism" Crane raises the ante.
Failure means death. Human behavior is seen as absurd for it often
places the protagonist in danger unnecessarily.

This story begins, as do many of Crane's war stories, with an over-
view of a battlefield. Shells from cannons are flying back and forth,
and rifle bullets are zipping to and fro. Many are wounded. In the
midst of this deadly situation, one soldier, Fred Collins, declares
loudly, "Thunder, I wisht I had a drink. Ain't there any water round
here?" (6:48). His fellows joke with him: "Well, if yeh want a drink so
bad, why don't you git it?" (6:50). They badger him until he asks his
Captain for permission "to go git some water from that there well over
yonder!" Trying to dissuade Collins, the captain states the crux of the
story: "Don't you think that's taking pretty big risks for a little drink
of water?" (6:52). Collins replies "dumbly," but is unpersuaded. Con-
ferring with a colonel, the Captain finally tells Collins to take "some
of the other boys' canteens with you an' hurry back now" (6:52).

Collins cannot back down now, although he finally realizes his stu-
pidity: dazed, he "appear[s] as a man in a dream" (6:52), and prepares
to cross no-man's land:

> When Collins faced the meadow and walked away from the regi-
> ment, he was vaguely conscious that a chasm, the deep valley of all
> prides, was suddenly between him and his comrades. It was provi-
> sional, but the provision was that he return as victor. He had blindly
> been led by quaint emotions and laid himself under an obligation to
> walk squarely up to the face of death. . . .
>   Too, he wondered why he did not feel some keen agony of fear. . . .
> He wondered at this because human expression had said loudly for
> centuries that men should feel afraid of certain things and that all
> men who did not feel this fear were phenomena, heroes.
>   He was then a hero. He suffered that disappointment which we
> would all have if we discovered that we were ourselves capable of
> those deeds which we most admire in history and legend. This,
> then, was a hero. (6:53)

He then decides that he is not a hero, for heroes lead unsullied lives. Collins, recalling that he had once avoided paying a debt, believes himself to be "an intruder in the land of fine deeds," but he perseveres. With the sky "full of fiends who directed all their wild rage at his head," he fills the canteens and a bucket, and starts back, pausing only to give a drink to a soldier lying mortally wounded on the field. Leaving the canteens, Collins returns with the bucket and is himself unscathed. He receives a roar of welcome from the regiment and then cries of derision as it is discovered that the bucket is empty. The story is an examination of the difference between illusion and reality, between misperceptions and perceptions that are dimmed by shock, by wondering how one got in a given position. The significance of Collins's action is as empty as the bucket; the "mystery" of his "heroism" is resolved by the recognition that egotism, pride, and saving face are at the heart of many, if not all, deeds commonly perceived as heroic.

In "An Indiana Campaign," the face-saving incident derives from the role played by an old man, Major Tom Boldin, the only man in town to have been in a war. It is a slight, humorous story of a small Indiana town, Migglesville, and its encounter with what it thinks is a "rebel." It begins as an adult version of "Lynx-Hunting." Major Boldin, who served in the Mexican War, and who consequently becomes the town's leader during this crisis, goes after a "rebel" who had stolen a few chickens and run into the woods. The Major retrieves an old, smooth-bored rifle from its position over a fireplace mantel and, with Peter Witheby behind him, strides into the woods to capture the enemy. After much fussing, fuming, and hesitation, they find not an enemy but a drunken citizen, "ol' Milt' Jacoby" (6:66). The story makes fun of small towns and of communities everywhere, and also of the war-time hysteria on the home front.

Crane makes interesting use of chickens in an extended metaphor that prefigures the behavior of the townsfolk, who pretend to be brave. At the beginning of the story, "an extremely excited" boy runs across a road to tell the Major, sleeping on a chair next to a building, about the "rebel": "He gave a shrill whoop . . . and rushed toward [the major]. He created a terrific panic among some chickens who had been scratching near the major's feet. They clamored in an insanity of fear and rushed hither and thither seeking a way to escape, whereas in reality all ways lay plainly open to them. . . . Meanwhile, some clever chicken had discovered a passage to safety and led the flock into the garden where they squawked in sustained alarm" (6:57–58). The women and the children, like the chickens, huddle and clamor in an insanity of fear, and rush hither and thither upon seeing anyone, friend or enemy, moving in the woods. In reality, all ways of escape lay plainly open to them. The men simply are little boys playing at war.

One of the stories in *The Little Regiment*, "The Veteran," seems out of place, for its only connections to war are that the protagonist is Henry Fleming, the "youth" of *The Red Badge of Courage* now grown old, and that it provides a kind of afterword to the novel.[60] In the first half of the story, readers learn that Fleming survived the war, that the battle described in the novel "was at Chancellorsville," that he had been promoted to sergeant, and that he had learned, as *The Red Badge* suggests, "to put the sin [of desertion] at a distance." He no longer seems ashamed of having deserted, and speaks of it openly: "I thought they were all shooting at me. Yes, Sir. . . . So I run!" (6:83). The second half describes Fleming's death. His barn catches fire, and in a successful attempt to save his hired hand and his horses, he loses his own life.

The critical problem in interpreting the story lies in the last paragraph: "When the roof fell in, a great funnel of smoke swarmed toward the sky, as if the old man's mighty spirit, released from its body—a little bottle—had swelled like the genie of fable. The smoke was tinted rose-hue from the flames, and perhaps the unutterable midnights of the universe will have no power to daunt the color of his soul" (6:86). It would be pleasant to believe that such a gentle, heroic, and long-suffering man had received a kind of immortality. And as people still read this story more than one hundred years after it was written, it could be said that he has achieved, with Crane, a kind of immortality. Within the frame of the story itself, however, there is little to suggest that Henry Fleming is any different from any of Crane's other protagonists. The very lyricism of the last paragraph implies a comparison to the lyrical endings of Crane's other stories, and *The Red Badge*, "The Bride Comes to Yellow Sky," "The Blue Hotel," and "The Open Boat" (to name only the most accomplished stories) are held by many critics to end ironically.[61] The conclusion, then, is that whenever Crane is most lyrical, he is also most ironic, and that Henry Fleming does not, despite the lyric beauty of the closing passage, achieve immortality.

The Little Regiment, while containing no outstanding story, does present something of a bridge between the apprentice Crane of the early *Sullivan County Sketches* and the master Crane of the later great stories. On the one hand, he retains the naturalistic and parodic leanings of his early "clever" period; on the other, he is beginning to explore more deeply the consequence of meaningless action in an absurd universe.

"An Episode of War" was finished too late to be included in *The Little Regiment*, but had it been, it would have been the best story in the volume. Unlike most of the other Civil War stories, it concentrates on the individual—injured, bewildered, and alone—caught in the madness of war for which he no longer has any feelings. The war represents a universe that has little to do with the protagonist except that it can, quite by chance, annihilate him. The story begins with a lieutenant doling out his company's ration of coffee. He is good at it, but, "on the verge of a great triumph in mathematics," he is wounded in the arm by a bullet from an enemy rifle. The rest of the story tells of the lieutenant's retreat to the rear in search of a hospital.

His wound detaches him, isolates him from his fellow soldiers and even, strangely, from the war: an orderly sergeant, helping the officer replace his sword in its scabbard,

> did not allow even his finger to brush the body of the lieutenant. A wound gives a strange dignity to him who bears it. Well men shy from this new and terrible majesty. It is as if the wounded man's hand is upon the curtain which hangs before the revelation of all existence, the meaning of ants, potentates, wars, cities, sunshine, snow, a feather dropped from a bird's wing, and the power of it sheds radiance upon a bloody form, and makes the men understand sometimes that they are little. . . . As the wounded officer passed from the line of battle, he was able to see many things which as a participant in the fight were unknown to him. (6:90)

As he moves farther toward the rear, he is helped by an officer who redresses the wound incompetently. Continuing on his way, he comes across a surgeon who says, "come along with me and I'll tend to it" (6:92). The lieutenant expresses concern about whether he will lose the arm; the surgeon says "Nonsense! . . . I won't amputate it" (6:92). The story closes by stating, "this is the story of how the lieutenant lost his arm" (6:93).

The casual quality of the story shocks somehow. The unlucky wound, the offhand return to the rear, the careless lie of the surgeon, and the self-deprecating response of the lieutenant to his family's cries of concern: "Oh, well, . . . I don't suppose it matters so much as that" (6:93) all point to the indifference of war. Maintaining a casual or indifferent stance is a way to shy away from being reminded that men are "little" and mortal.

Crane first saw battle in 1897, when he went to Greece to report on the Greco-Turkish War from the perspective of the losing side. This experience greatly improved his ability to write short stories about war, and his war stories after *The Little Regiment* are both more believable and more aesthetically pleasing. "Death and the Child" (5:121–41) is characteristic of the war fiction he could now write. It has much in common with "The Open Boat," which was also based on a real experience, and shares its themes of the indifference of nature and the horror and pity of death.

The protagonist, Peza, is an Italian of Greek heritage, who comes to Greece as a spectator, but, learning the pull of heritage, he soon joins the fight. Initially, Peza is confounded by the chaos of war, in contrast to an officer with whom he moves toward the front. The officer is "stern, quiet, and confident"; Peza is excitable, noisy, and confused. This officer responds to Peza's excitement with the "vanity of experience." Egotistical as any child in the Whilomville stories, Peza nevertheless responds to authority with unquestioning acceptance, just as any of those children do, and consequently becomes as insignificant as anyone else in the war. Peza is quickly initiated into battle. Inheriting a rifle from one dead man and a cartridge belt from another, he is ready to fight. But in taking on the accoutrements of the dead, he comes closer to them. Seeing horror in the eyes of the dead men, he cannot take it any longer, and he runs away.

The story is about consciousness, a realization of truth. Peza encounters a man, a "spectre" with his jaw "half shot away." Like all other people in Crane's fiction he is afraid of the men in the procession of wounded: "even Peza's fingers revolted; he was afraid even to touch" the wounded man. The setting and the metaphors reinforce the notion of a descent into unconsciousness and a rise to greater consciousness. Running from the wounded, Peza gains "the top of a great hill" from which he can observe the battle far below: he sees "little black lines" and "slanted sheets of smoke." Still excited, he "bounds" down the hill into hell. As he gazes at the carnage, he learns that "pity had a numerical limit." Near the "bottom of the abyss"—that is, in Hell—Peza has a strange vision of the battle in which the world is turned upside down: "In the vale there was an effect as if one was then beneath the battle. . . . Alone, unguided, Peza felt like a man groping in a cellar" (5:130). He reaches the bottom of the pit, and staring at a dead man, feels himself "drawn by these dead men slowly, firmly down as to some mystic chamber under the earth" (5:139). Unable to distinguish between his hallucinations and reality, Peza runs back up and away from the battle until he reaches high ground. Encountering a child abandoned in the war "on a mountain," Peza seems to have returned from Hell, to have reached the mountain top. But the child's question, "Are you a man?" undercuts any sense of relief, any sense of having moved away from death into permanent safety. Peza realizes his insignificance and reflects that "the definition of his misery could be written on a wee grass-blade" (5:141). It is here that Peza learns what the character Vernall expresses in "War Memories": War "is simply life."

In Cuba in 1898, Crane got much closer to battle than he had in Greece, so much so that he was shot at, acted as a courier, and contracted the yellow fever that killed more American soldiers than did the enemy. After his Cuban experience, Crane returned with renewed vigor to war as a subject, producing a collection of eleven short stories entitled *Wounds in the Rain*: "The Price of the Harness," "The Lone Charge of William B. Perkins," "The Clan of No-Name," " 'God Rest Ye, Merry Gentlemen,' " "The Revenge of the *Adolphus*," "The Sergeant's Private Mad-house," "Virtue in War," "Marines Signalling Under Fire at Guantánamo," "This Majestic Lie," "War Memories," and "The Second Generation." All are stories about the Spanish-American War. Although Crane claimed that seeing war merely confirmed the earlier assumptions of his imagination—"The Red Badge is all right," he said after reporting the Greco-Turkish War—some technical advances are evident in these later stories.

The quality of these stories varies greatly. Some are only slightly reworked versions of journalistic accounts. One suspects that they were written solely for money, and written quickly because he was sick. " 'God Rest Ye, Merry Gentlemen' " (6:137–54), "Marines Signalling Under Fire at Guantanamo" (6:194–200), and "This Majestic Lie" (6:201–21) are barely fictional accounts of Crane's and others' experiences toward the end and after the end of hostilities in Cuba. "The Lone Charge of William B. Perkins" (6:114–18) is "A Mystery of Heroism" in a Cuban setting, with one important difference: in "The Lone Charge," no one is around to congratulate Perkins on his safe return from almost certain death. Consequently, the absurdity of the situation is more striking; had Perkins died, no one would have noticed or cared. Absurdity is also central to "The Sergeant's Private Mad-house"

(6:172–79). A thoroughly frightened soldier almost brings disaster on himself and his company by imagining an imminent Spanish attack, and thus causing panic. Later, when the Spaniards do attack, the mad soldier's singing saves him and his company. This is the same irony of chance evident in "The Five White Mice."

"The Revenge of the *Adolphus*" (6:155–71) is an interesting experiment in chance and truth. The story involves six ships: two Spanish gunboats; an unarmed American despatch boat, the *Adolphus*, carrying war correspondents; one big American cruiser, the *Chancellorville*; and two American gunboats, which are a refitted yacht, the *Holy Moses*, and a tug, the *Chicken*. The story opens like "One Dash—Horses": the *Adolphus* is cruising and minding its own business, when, by chance, it crosses the path of the Spanish gunboats, which then pursue her. Gradually losing ground, the *Adolphus* comes across the *Chancellorville*, just as Richardson and José had chanced upon the Federales. After a brief battle, the Spanish boats are sunk, and on the *Chicken*, one man is killed and four wounded. The *Adolphus* goes to Key West, where the correspondents make their reports.

The *Adolphus* has her revenge in two ways. Naturally, having been chased by some very determined Spaniards, the *Adolphus* later becomes instrumental in the sinking of the Spanish boats. On another level, however, revenge consists of the stories the correspondents write in which the big ship, important to those at home, is virtually ignored as never having been endangered. The *Chancellorville*, on the sea at least, is as big and impersonal as was the Battle of Chancellorsville on which Crane is said to have based *The Red Badge*. A yacht and a tug are to the cruiser as are privates to generals: "When the officers of the noble squadron [of American ships in the Caribbean, specifically, of the *Chancellorville*], received the newspapers containing an account of their performance, they looked at each other somewhat dejectedly: 'Heroic assault—grand daring of Boatswain Pent [of the *Chicken*]—superb accuracy of the *Holy Moses*' fire—gallant tars of the *Chicken*—their names should be remembered as long as America stands . . .'" (6:171).

The point is that Crane's experience had confirmed him in his belief that a phoney heroism is created by the good press coverage big things, such as regiments and battle cruisers, receive. True heroism, in contrast, is the sole property of small things, such as individuals and small boats. With this story, Crane had his revenge on those who sat safely at Key West and reported the war in Cuba. He also had his revenge on the Navy Department: "When the Secretary of the Navy ultimately read the report of Commander Surrey, S.O.P. [of the *Chancellorville*], he had to prick himself with a dagger in order to remember that anything at all out of the ordinary had occurred" (6:171).

The "yellow" press of the day made much of the sword-waving, charge-inciting, gentleman-officer and his supposed heroics. In "The Second Generation," Crane criticizes this kind of journalism and this kind of person. Caspar Cadogan (Cad again?), son of a United States senator, decides he wants to go to war. He thinks he wants to fight, to be in charge of a company or more. The senator gets him a commission as a captain, but as captain of the commissariat, that part of an army charged with supplying food and drink for the soldiers. Caspar fails at his job miserably. He also happens to get involved in the charge up San Juan Hill. He acquits himself reasonably well—he does go up, although without waving his sword. Once trapped there, however, the soldiers are without food and drink. Caspar, it seems, is the only soldier around with a full canteen of water. He hides it for a while, but is found out. Meanwhile the senator pulls strings to get his son leave to come home. During a discussion, the senator discovers that Caspar does not want to stay in the army, although the senator believes he could make Caspar a general in seven or eight years. Having failed at everything else, it seems that Caspar has failed in the military, too. The senator, reprehensible for his own nepotism, replies, "I guess you are no damn good" (6:284). He is right, but not because Caspar does not want a career in the army, but because he is the selfish prig he was raised to be.

Willa Cather said that "The Price of the Harness" (6:97–113) "just misses being a fine story."[62] In fact, it is finer than she suggests. The story appears to contain a new element in Crane's writing: a genuine love for and solidarity of the group. At the beginning there are four companions, common soldiers limited in perception. Unlike Crane's earlier heroes, these men are not heroic because they manage to apprehend the reality of their own insignificance; they already know that they are insignificant. They are heroic because, in spite of the danger, they simply perform their duty. The group is separated by injury: Martin, wounded in the arm, moves to the rear (as do many of Crane's soldiers, including the lieutenant in "An Episode of War"); Watkins is mortally wounded—shot in the lung; Grierson gets yellow fever; and Nolan, shot in the stomach, dies on the field.

It is easy to see little or no irony in Nolan's thoughts as he and his fellows charge up a hill: "He sprang to his feet and, stooping, ran with the others. Something fine, soft, gentle, touched his heart as he ran. He loved the regiment, the army, because the regiment, the army, was his life. He had no other outlook; and now these men, his comrades, were performing his dream-scenes for him. They were doing as he had ordained. . . . His part, to his mind, was merely that of going along with the crowd" (6:110). Given the easy comradeship of the four men, it is tempting to believe that Crane's views have changed, that the group now is important. But Crane's "irony of soul" asserts itself at the end of the story, where, in the yellow-fever tent, a wounded man sings, ironically, the "Star Spangled Banner," his song interspersed with the voice of another soldier relating the gruesome death of Nolan. There is also irony at the beginning of the story, although more subtly portrayed: "From time to time a government pack-train, led by a sleek-sided tender bell-mare, came from one way or the other way, and the men stood aside as the strong, hard, black-and-tan animals crowded eagerly after their curious little feminine leader." As Crane insists in a letter to his agent on retaining the title he gave to the story, "The name of the story is 'The Price of the Harness' because it *is* the price of the harness, the price the men paid for wearing the military harness, Uncle Sam's military harness; and they paid blood, hunger and fever."[63] Mules and men in harness are the same. Nolan's action, like that of the mules, "was merely that of going along with the crowd." As it is difficult to take the singing of the national anthem in any way but ironically, one must conclude that Crane has not changed his views of the group, but rather gained a new insight into heroism as an individual act of simply performing one's "duty." Moreover, as the description of the mules is related to that of the men, even this new insight into heroism is not unmixed with Crane's skepticism.

"Virtue in War" (6:180–93) takes Crane's new-found discovery that heroism consists in men doing their jobs and applies it to a professional soldier, Major Gates, a West Pointer, formerly of the "Sixteenth Cavalry," now retired. Gates is "highly educated," like the coward Caspar of "The Second Generation," but unlike Caspar, Gates also is "strictly military." Gates's first job is to make soldiers of his men, who, like most of the Americans who shuffled down to Cuba, had never seen an army uniform. They grumble at the work and the drills, but Gates molds them into a crack battalion. Gates is contrasted with "Major Rickets C. Carmony," whose greatest claim to fame is that he was "one of the biggest wholesale hardware dealers in his State" (6:181). Carmony is very popular—he serves his men ice-cream; Gates, initially, is

not—he serves them hard work. Many of Gates's superiors are ama-
teurs, and he is surrounded by people who do not know their business.
Once in battle Gates's men perform almost as well as the regular soldiers and much better than Carmony's regiment. During the fight,
Gates is wounded, and he bleeds to death.

Crane's irony closes the story in the form of a conversation between
war correspondents, presumably the same newspaper men who appear
in "The Revenge of the *Adolphus*":

> Shackles was babbling plaintively about mint-juleps. . . .
>
> "By the way," said one at last, "it's too bad about poor old Gates
> of the 307th. He bled to death. His men were crazy. . . . When they
> got back there to look for him they found him just about gone, and
> another wounded man was trying to stop the flow with his hat! His
> hat, mind you. Poor old Gatesie!"
>
> "Oh, no, Shackles!" said the third man of the party. "Oh, no;
> you're wrong. The best mint-juleps in the world are made right in
> New York, Philadelphia or Boston." (6:192)

Just as Nolan's death is related while the national anthem is being sung
in "The Price of the Harness," the description of the death of Gates is
interspersed with an argument about mint juleps in "Virtue in War."

"War Memories" (6:222–63) is written in the first person, a characteristic of Crane's journalism that provoked many parodies.[64] "War
Memories" is probably a fictionalized account of Crane's own experiences: the hero closely resembles Crane, and Vernall, the name of the
protagonist, is close to "vernal," meaning "green" or inexperienced,
which Crane was. Vernall moves from innocence to experience, as do
many of Crane's characters. He boards a ship and engages in a silly,
gratuitous "war" with a bunch of bananas hung by another correspondent in the middle of their sleeping quarters. He sees several dead men,
and finally returns home, having contracted yellow fever.

"War Memories" begins with the same recognition with which many
previous stories had ended: " 'But to get the real thing!' cried Vernall,
the war correspondent. 'It seems impossible!' " (6:222). In this story,
misperception is taken for granted; even Vernall knows that everyone
misperceives. Crane no longer rails against those trying to create false
order out of chaos, no longer believes that he can discover meaning,
"the real thing," the essence of the war, in the temporary apprehension
of reality in a fragment of time. The episodes of this story do not build
toward such an apprehension. Instead, the story comprises a series of

episodes in which trying to apprehend reality is almost half-hearted. It is impossible to get the real thing in war "because war is simply life, and an expression of life can always evade us" (6:222). No longer overtly concerned with impressionist descriptions (although they do appear because they came naturally), Crane now provides a series of events designed for a cumulative effect. No one of these will get the real thing, but perhaps in the accumulation there will be something. The story of the bananas is a metaphor for all that follows.

> But the bunch did not become really aggressive until we were well at sea. Then it began to spar. With the first roll of the ship, it launched its bulk at McCurdy and knocked him wildly through the door to the deck-rail, where he hung cursing hysterically. Without a moment's pause, it made for me. I flung myself head-first into my bunk and watched the demon sweep Brownlow into a corner and wedge his knee behind a sea-chest. Kary gave a shrill cry and fled. The bunch of bananas swung to and fro . . . looking for more men. . . . You see? War! A bunch of bananas rampant because the ship rolled. (6:222)

That is, something bigger than individuals—a ship—had moved, and purely by chance, that movement had caused mayhem in a ship's cabin or, in effect, a war. All the death and destruction seen by Vernall must be viewed from this perspective: "the war. . . . was not a gory giant; it was a bunch of bananas swung in the middle of a cabin" (6:223).

Vernall's first view of death comes after the landing and a night-time skirmish during which Vernall's friend, the ship's surgeon, Gibbs, is killed. The language is so lean, spare, and unemotional, even while describing a dying man, that it seems to parody the prose style of Ernest Hemingway, who was born in 1899, the year "War Memories" was published: "I heard somebody dying near me. He was dying hard. . . . I thought this man would never die. I wanted him to die. Ultimately, he died." Vernall's realization that he wishes a man dead is chilling to the reader, but his cold indifference following Gibbs's death is even more disturbing: "At that moment, the adjutant came bustling along. . . . 'Where's the doctor?' . . . 'Just died this minute, sir.' . . . Despite the horror of this night's business, the man's mind was somehow influenced by the coincidence of the adjutant's calling aloud for the doctor within a few seconds of the doctor's death. It—what shall I say—It interested him, this coincidence" (6:227). War and death simply are parts of life.

Crane's new admiration for men doing their duty, even collectively doing their duty as part of a group, becomes most apparent in his un-ambiguous praise of such people as those in "War Memories." It is not that he suddenly believes in the solidarity of the group; it is rather that the group behaves well for no apparent reason. Even the mild irony of "The Price of the Harness" is gone, replaced by Vernall's—and Crane's—conviction that "The fine thing about 'the men' is that you can't explain them. I mean when you take them collectively. They do a thing, and afterward you find that they have done it because they have done it" (6:230). Vernall sees "one truly Romantic figure," a Cuban officer "posing like a statue of victory"; "But outside of this splendid person it was simply a picture of men at work" (6:231). And later, having returned to the despatch-boat, he says that "War is death, and a plague of the lack of small things, and toil" (6:235).

In the closing pages of the story, Vernall describes his ignorance of events. He says "We did not know" twice, and "I did not understand," "I would not know," "I mistook," "I could not understand," and "I don't know" (6:237–39). When the scenes move away from the battle, details blur, and there follow several pages describing confusion and chaos. Nobody knows much of anything. The story ends with the narrator's statement that "you may depend on it that I have told you nothing at all, nothing at all, nothing at all" (6:263), a recognition that the only certainty is a lack of certainty.

"The Clan of No-Name" (6:119–36) is a story similar to "The Price of the Harness" in its seeming glorification of the group, and like "War Memories" in the casual way the living respond to the dead. The story begins with Margharita allowing herself to be courted by Mr. Smith, having decided to two-time Manolo Prat. Then Manolo's first battle, his considerable bravery, and his death are described. The story ends by returning to Margharita and Mr. Smith, who loves her desperately. He proposes and she accepts. That night, she burns Prat's photograph.

Just as Prat's story is enclosed by the story of Margharita and Smith, so both stories are enclosed by riddles. Between the title and the first line comes this riddle: "Unwind my riddle. / Cruel as hawks the hours fly, / Wounded men seldom come home to die, / The hard waves see an arm flung high, / Scorn hits strong because of a lie, / yet there exists a mystic tie. / Unwind my riddle" (6:119). The last paragraph reads like another riddle: "For the word is clear only to the kind who on peak or plain, from dark northern ice-fields to the hot wet jungles, through all wine and want, through lies and unfamiliar truth, dark or light, are governed by the unknown gods, and though each man knows the law no man may give tongue to it" (6:136). What is that word, the answer to that riddle? There is no clear answer. It may be "love" in the message Prat had written on his picture. It may be the treachery of Margharita. It may be, ironically, a love that encompasses the likelihood of betrayal. In describing Smith's feelings for Margharita, the narrator states, "It was part of his love to believe in the absolute treachery of his adored one" (6:134). It may be both words or neither. Probably, the clear word that everyone knows but to which "no man may give tongue" is "absurdity" or "meaninglessness" or "pathos" or "death," for it is also clear that death is final, ending everything—even love. There is a mystic tie between life and death, but life, although inextricably bound to death, also scorns it, even denies it when it can.

Spitzbergen Tales, a group of stories about the twelfth regiment of a mythical army, was written during the year or so before Crane's death. Given how ill he was and how deep in debt, it is remarkable that these stories are so spare (he was paid by the word), so pessimistic (tubercular people tend to have visions of grand enterprises at the end), and that any of them is any good at all. And one, "The Upturned Face," is very good indeed.

The University Press of Virginia Edition of *The Works of Stephen Crane* places these stories, with good biographical support, in an order approximating that of the dates of their composition: first, "The Kicking Twelfth"; second, "The Upturned Face"; third, "The Shrapnel of Their Friends"; and last, "'And If He Wills We Must Die.'" Viewed as a composite novel, however, one in which each successive story narrows the focus from the general to the specific, the stories should be arranged in a different order, with "The Upturned Face" moved to the end. "The Kicking Twelfth" (6:287–96) has, as Holton says, "a whole regiment as protagonist" (267). "The Shrapnel of Their Friends" (6:301–6) has the same regiment, much reduced by death and injury, as protagonist. "'And If He Wills, We Must Die'" (6:307–12) reduces the focus to sixteen people, and "The Upturned Face" (6:297–300) concentrates on a dead man and the two men who bury him. Following this order, it is clear that the first stories focus on big groups, and, consequently, see little. As the stories in the collection begin to focus on less, they see more, get closer to "the real thing."

"The Kicking Twelfth" introduces "young Timothy Lean, a second-lieutenant in the First Company of the third battalion" (6:288), but the main character is really the regiment. The regiment is shown acquitting itself well in its first engagement. In fact, the regiment and the reader seem to be lulled into the story by a fairly generalized, long-distance view of war. Lean leads his men up an almost impossibly steep hill, and the Spanish abandon their superior position. Lean is first to reach the top, and the story ends with the colonel's praise: "Lean, you young whelp, you—you're a good boy" (6:296). "The Shrapnel of Their Friends" picks up where "Kicking" leaves off, with "a general admission that the Kicking Twelfth had taken the chief honors of the day" (6:301)—but not without a price. So many officers had been killed that Lean has been given a company: "It was not too much of a company. Fifty-three smudged and sweating men . . ." (6:302). The battle continues, and the Twelfth regains a position, but is mistaken for the enemy by its own battery some distance away. When the shrapnel begins to fall on them, they retreat. The general curses them until he discovers the cause of their retreat.

In "'And If He Wills, We Must Die,'" Lean is absent. In his place and in place of an entire regiment are "a serjeant, a corporal, and four-teen men of the Twelfth" (6:307). They are sent to occupy a house situated on a main road, at least half a mile ahead of their lines. On the road, the old soldier, Sergeant Morton, contrasts the quality of the army of the old days with that of today's, to the detriment of the latter. Barely settled in the house, they are attacked. In the first exchange of fire, one soldier in the house is shot in the throat. No reaction from the men is reported. Soon another man is killed so undramatically that no one sees him being shot. Three more men are wounded, and they are told to make themselves useful somehow. When or how they were wounded is not reported. Corporal Flagler is shot. A man suggests to Morton that they run away. Then he is killed. Another man is wounded. Then Morton is killed. The skirmish ends when the enemy enters the house. In this story, death has come a lot closer to the regiment and to the reader. Instead of a regiment, there are individuals. To say that a regiment is wiped out produces sadness, but to say that "Corporal Flagler is shot" produces a response much more genuine, for the reader had begun to know Corporal Flagler.

Comprising fewer than two thousand words, "The Upturned Face" is perhaps Crane's leanest, sparest story. After reading it, one is positive that bullets are whizzing constantly around the men, but a careful examination reveals that bullets are mentioned only twice. Partly because of this excruciating economy, "The Upturned Face" is an extremely modern, even postmodern story. The plot is simple: Timothy Lean and an adjutant bury a dead officer. Beginning in *The Red Badge* and running through dozens of stories, Crane's protagonists avoid the great horror of death. Whole regiments walk around dead bodies, wounded men are avoided like plagues, the dead are feared so much that no one wants to touch them. Richardson, in "One Dash—Horses," fears to touch even a blanket behind which is a room containing men who want to kill him. Peza, in "Death and the Child," cannot bring himself to touch a wounded man. This horror is, in part, the same horror the good citizens see reflected in the faceless idiocy of Henry Johnson. Like the blanket in "One Dash—Horses," the dead soldiers and the faceless Johnson are horrible emblems of death and horrible in themselves. No one wants to be reminded of his insignificance. Having walked around and around the issue of death for years, Crane faced it most convincingly in "The Upturned Face." The story begins with the fact of death, which is where most of Crane's work leaves off: "'What will we do now?' said the adjutant" (6:297). Most of Crane's protagonists ask this question at the end of their stories, and the answer is projected beyond the frame of the story, but this time there is an answer: "'Bury him,' said Timothy Lean."

Given Crane's career-long penchant for odd details in descriptions of death—arms at peculiar angles, gaping wounds in throats, blood running in rivulets down parts of bodies—it is surprising that this story lacks them. The narrator briefly mentions "blood-stained buttons," but keeps the focus on the dead man's face, describing it sparely with one detail: it is "chalk-blue" (6:297, 299, 300). And yet this lack of details evokes more horror than does Crane's usual practice. The story is bizarre, perhaps even expressionistic, "pure symbol," as Berryman says.[65] Face-down or avoided, dead men may be ignored, as may death, but "up-turned," the faces of the dead demand a reaction. The face of the Swede is up-turned: his dead eyes gaze at a cash register. The eyes of a dead man in "Death and the Child" pull Peza down to Hell. Even Henry Johnson's face must have been turned upward for the acid to drip onto it from a table. In "The Upturned Face," however, Crane focuses solely on one man's reaction to the face of death.

We are used to the absence of other details, the spare settings and plots characteristic of Crane's stories. The setting could be anywhere, although readers of other stories know it must be Cuba. There are only two names: "Timothy Lean" and "Bill," the dead man. The enemy, which has "the exact range" of Lean's position, is invisible. The entire action concentrates on this simple burial under fire. In spite of the danger (bullets "snap" and "spit"), there is a job to be done: the body must be buried. Two enlisted men, unnamed, are asked to dig the grave. Neither Lean nor the adjutant wants to touch the body. The adjutant forces Lean to empty the pockets of personal things. Although the enlisted men could be made to "tumble him in," the job is accepted by Lean: "I suppose . . . it would be better if we laid him in ourselves" (6:298). Although they manage to look at the face, like Crane's other characters, they avoid touching him: "Both were particular that their fingers should not feel the corpse"; rather, "they took hold of the dead officer's clothing." Looking at death, it seems, is easier than touching it.[66]

The adjutant remembers that some words should be said over the grave. Again Lean does the deed, the adjutant contributing a word or two. Neither can remember the entire service, and so they leave off after a while. One soldier begins to fill in the grave, but, after shoveling some mud on the feet, he is wounded, and both enlisted men are sent to the rear and out of the story. Lean finishes the job, but not before making "a gesture of abhorrence." Working frantically, he covers nearly everything: "Soon there was nothing to be seen but the chalk-blue face." Horrified by the face, the two argue for a bit. Finally, "Lean swung back the shovel; it went forward in a pendulum curve. When the earth landed it made a sound—plop." In other stories, upturned faces are seen momentarily, quickly avoided, and then the living move on. In "The Upturned Face," it is the last thing they see.

Crane was among the first American Impressionists and Naturalists, and he was also among the first Expressionists. Expressionism, partly a reaction against impressionism and partly an articulation of nihilism,[67] avoids the rational, attempting instead to voice the emotions of hope, dread, and horror, using "distortion, exaggeration that ends in caricature, and a brutal, slashing color."[68] Because of its brutality, its flat characters, and the "chalk-blue" face that keeps thrusting itself into the story, "The Upturned Face" may be seen as an expressionistic response to the horror of death in a meaningless universe.

A typical response to horror in expressionistic fiction is one of ritual.

"What do we do now?" "Bury him." And they do. Exposing themselves to the accurate fire of the enemy, Lean and the others dig a grave, lay the dead man in the grave, stand at attention beside the grave trying to speak the funeral service, and cover the grave with dirt. Ritual is a way of creating order out of chaos, a way of giving comfort and meaning, even as it creates horror and, in this case, danger. Lean must look into the face, even as he covers it with dirt. The importance of this ritual is made all the more evident by its absurdity and the fact of the bullets constantly threatening death to the living. It is a ritual without pretension: unlike Whilomville's rituals of cruelty, it performs a kindness; unlike the town's innumerable rituals of self-protection, this one is fraught with danger. Unlike the tedious tea parties of the women and the barber-shop banalities of the men, this ritual is genuine, both forcing and enabling Lean to face the horror. Accepting ritual, in Crane's view, is not easy. Death remains horrible—ritual does not lessen its horror—but ritual enables one to face it.

It is always risky to speculate about what someone might have done, especially when regarding a writer such as Stephen Crane. Crane began his writing career, as Howells said, nearly "fully armed"; he had the "angle," as James Dickey says, and had it at the beginning. Even so, it has been said that his early death probably was no loss to literature, that he was producing only hack work at the end, and that he had gone as far as he could go. Even Joseph Conrad, Crane's friend and admirer, said of him that he was "the *only* Impressionist . . . and *only* an Impressionist."[69] Others, like Gullason, while admiring parts of some late stories, believe that illness and debt caused Crane to capitalize on his demand as a newspaperman so that his late work was too journalistic, too self-conscious, editorializing, and hurried.[70]

While it is true that much of his late work is not his best, and that his sense of the absurd, his impressionism and symbolism, and his recognition of limited vision were evident at the beginning of his career, Crane was at the end sloughing off the excess. He grew toward economy, toward a more gemlike expression of meaninglessness.

The old central problem remained: to find a response to that meaninglessness. Stephen Crane was beginning to find an answer. He was beginning in such late stories as "Death and the Child" and especially "The Upturned Face" to find in ritual a meaningful answer, to move toward a notion of courage as "grace under pressure," and toward a feeling that ritual could provide a means for acting under pressure, perhaps the *only* means of acting gracefully under pressure. Lean's ritual in "The Upturned Face" does not change the fact of an absurd universe, but it describes a method of dealing with it. Death is still to be feared, but death, too, is absurd. The only thing meaningful is how one reacts to death, how one behaves in the face of it.

A story related third-hand by the biographer R. W. Stallman tells of Crane and other journalists huddling behind an earthen bunker at Guantánamo during the Cuban war. The bunker was receiving heavy fire from rifles when "suddenly Crane, who was incapable of bravado, let himself quietly over the redoubt, lighted a cigarette, stood for a few moments with his arms at his sides, while the bullets hissed past him into the mud, then as quietly climbed back over the redoubt and strolled away."[71] To the extent that, for Crane, smoking was a habit—and therefore a kind of ritual—the story tells much about Crane's belief that the rituals of life allow one to look into the face of death: "war is simply life."

Crane's late fiction was beginning to reflect a new and more profound vision. He had spent his writing career walking around corpses, avoiding upturned faces. At the end, he faced them, and, had he lived the normal span, he might have led the next generation of American writers in their battles instead of preparing the field for them.

Notes

1. *Stephen Crane: Tales, Sketches, and Reports*, Vol. 8, *The University of Virginia Edition of The Works of Stephen Crane*, ed. Fredson Bowers (Charlottesville: University Press of Virginia, 1973), 771: "If a note by Cora [Crane's common-law wife] written in the upper left corner of the manuscript can be trusted, Uncle Jake and the Bell-Handle was written when Crane was fourteen years old, that is, in 1885." Subsequent notes refer to the edition as *"Works."*

2. Letter 169, to John Northern Hilliard, 2 January 1896, *The Correspondence of Stephen Crane*, ed. Stanley Wertheim and Paul Sorrentino (New York: Columbia University Press, 1988), 1:167. Hereafter cited as *Correspondence.*

3. Schoberlin, who in 1949 published ten of Crane's stories of this period, called them "Sullivan County Sketches," and the name has stuck, probably because it is a good one.

4. See Edwin H. Cady, introduction to *Works*, 7:xxii–xxxii.

5. Published in *Last Words*, 1902, "The Mesmeric Mountain," seems to have been written much earlier as "A Tale of Sullivan County." See *Works*, 8:860–61.

6. Letter 240, to the Editor of *Demorest's Family Magazine*, late April–early May 1896, *Correspondence*, 1:230, 231.

7. Appearing in February 1892, "The Last of the Mohicans" may have been the first of the "Sullivan County Sketches."

8. It is impossible, of course, to determine exactly the order in which Crane wrote most of these sketches, but given that they were submitted to newspapers, it is not too presumptuous to assume that those appearing later in 1892 were probably written after those published earlier that year.

9. J. C. Levenson, introduction to *Works*, 5:xx.

10. James Nagel, *Stephen Crane and Literary Impressionism* (University Park: Pennsylvania State University Press, 1980), 43.

11. "Stephen Crane's Own Story" is widely anthologized, but appeared originally in the New York *Press*, 7 January 1897.

12. See Donna Gerstenberger, "'The Open Boat': Additional Perspective," *Modern Fiction Studies* 17 (Winter 1971–72):558, for a full discussion of existentialism in the story.

13. "The Veteran" ends this way, as do many other stories. Even *The Red Badge*, for which "The Veteran" is a sort of coda, ends lyrically—and ironically.

14. Letter 73, to the Reverend Thomas Dixon, January 1895, *Correspondence*, 1896.

15. The other two are "In the Tenderloin: A Duel Between an Alarm Clock and a Suicidal Purpose" (8:384–38) and "In the Tenderloin" (8:392–96).

16. Milne Holton, *Cylinder of Vision: The Fiction and Journalistic Writing of Stephen Crane* (Baton Rouge: Louisiana State University Press, 1972), 138.

17. Lars Åhnebrink, *Beginnings of Naturalism*, vol. 9 of *Essays and Studies in American Language and Literature*, ed. S. B. Liljegran (New York: Russell & Russell, 1950), 26.

18. *Works*, 8:590–600. But see also, Corwin Knapp Linson, *My Stephen Crane*, ed. Edwin H. Cady (Syracuse: Syracuse University Press, 1958), 65–70. Linson, an artist and a friend of Crane, had gone to Scranton with Stephen.

19. "In the Depths of a Coal Mine: First Draft," *Works*, 8:601–7.

20. This is perhaps the first instance in Crane's fiction of an "upturned face."

21. Quoted in Thomas Beer, *Stephen Crane: A Study in American Letters* (New York: Knopf, 1923), 359.

22. Letter 746, to Catherine Harris, 12 November 1896, *Correspondence*, 2: appendix A, 671.

23. Fredric Jameson, *The Political Unconscious: Narrative as a Socially Symbolic Act* (Ithaca, N.Y.: Cornell University Press, 1981), 188. See also Raymond Williams, *The Country and the City* (New York: Oxford University Press, 1973), 222–24.

24. See, for example, Granville Hicks, *The Great Tradition: An Interpretation of American Literature Since the Civil War*, rev. ed. (New York: Biblo and Tannen, 1967), 160.

25. [M. Solomon], "Stephen Crane: A Critical Study," *Masses and Mainstream* 9 (January 1956):25–42 and (March 1956): 31–47. This is, of course, distinct from legitimate Marxist criticism.

26. Holton, *Cylinder of Vision*, 282, passim.

27. *Works*, 8:409–20.

28. Edwin Cody "Stephen Crane and the Strenuous Life," *ELH* 28 (1961):382.

29. See, for example, "The Monster," (7:35 and 44). Sometimes, this function is served by campfires or tables. In "The Blue Hotel," the stove offers protection from the storm outside, and, ironically a kind of false protection to the Swede. In "The Stove," a Whilomville story, a child's stove is the center of an ironic parody of adult society, producing as it does an imitation and travesty of that society. That society, interestingly, in light of "The Monster," described as a tea party, is itself a travesty of human behavior. In Crane's earlier writing, tables seem to have some of this same symbolic force, but the symbolism is not exploited fully; rather tables seem to be used more to organize a scene than as symbols of groups. There is, for example, the table that seems to be an "altar" in "Four Men in a Cave"; the table in "A Ghoul's Accountant"; the wooden table in "The Reluctant Voyagers" that seems "immovable, as if the craft had been builded around it"; the "fire-circle" (8:255) in "The Cry of A Huckleberry Pudding: A Dim Study of Camping Experiences" (8:254–59); and of campfires in other Sullivan County Sketches. In either case, stoves and tables are what T. S. Eliot called "objective correlatives," physical entities that produce the equivalent of a particular emotion with the force of symbols.

30. Usually, blue represents the unknowable in Crane, and, sometimes, chaos. Here he seems to have chosen Melville's scheme of using white for that purpose.

31. Sister Mary Anthony Weinig, "Homeric Convention in 'The Blue Hotel,'" *Stephen Crane Newsletter* 2 (Spring 1968):6–8.

32. See also J. C. Levenson, introduction to *Works*, 5:nb, xli–xlii.

33. Teddy Roosevelt, soon to become president of the United States, admired Crane's work. He was not fond of "A Man and Some Others," however, writing to Crane, "Some day I want you to write another story of the frontiersman and the Mexican Greaser in which the frontiersman shall come out on top; it is more normal that way!" (Roosevelt to Crane, 18 August 1896, *Correspondence*, 1:249). Roosevelt, who once called Patrick Henry a "dirty little atheist," had peculiar notions about normality.

34. J. C. Levenson, introduction to *Works*, 7:xv.

35. One is reminded as well of Conrad's harlequin in *The Heart of Darkness*.

36. Among the many "nihilistic" readings of "The Monster," the latest is perhaps Michael D. Warner, "Value, Agency, and Stephen Crane's 'The Monster,'" *Nineteenth-Century Fiction* 40, no. 1 (June 1985):76–93.

37. Robert A. Morace, "Games, Play, and Entertainments in Stephen Crane's 'The Monster,'" *Studies in American Fiction* 9, no. 1 (1981):65–81, 78.

38. This is also Crane's point in "The Blue Hotel" when the Easterner almost accepts his responsibility but falls back to a communal response.

39. The only interesting sentence in the story is that in which readers of "The Monster" learn almost off-handedly about "the late gallant Henry Johnson" (7:185). Henry's death allows the Trescott family to re-enter Whilomville society.

40. Ibid., 79.

41. Letter 356, Conrad to Crane, 16 January 1898, *Correspondence*, 1:328.

42. William Dean Howells, *Academy* 60 (3 February 1901), 177.

43. See footnote to letter 334, *Correspondence*, 1:306.

44. *Works*, 7:xii.

45. Levenson, *Works*, 7:xi.

46. Eric Solomon, *Stephen Crane in England* (Columbus: Ohio State University Press, 1965), 202.

47. Thomas A. Gullason, ed., *Stephen Crane's Career: Perspectives and Evaluations* (New York: New York University Press, 1972), 483. Gullason does not attempt to explain exactly what significance emerges or in what order.

48. Ibid.

49. Holton, *Cylinder of Vision*, 213.

50. Ibid., 216; Nagel, *Literary Impressionism*, 123.

51. Holton, *Cylinder of Vision*, fn. 220–21; see also, Donald B. Gibson, *The Fiction of Stephen Crane* (Carbondale: Southern Illinois University Press, 1968); see also Leslie A. Fiedler, *Love and Death in the American Novel* (New York: Dell, 1966).

52. Holton, *Cylinder of Vision*, 219.

53. Some believe this story to have been called "A Little Pilgrimage." See *Works*, 7:255.

54. But see George Monteiro, "Whilomville as Judah: Crane's 'A Little Pilgrimage,'" *Renascence* 19 (Summer 1967):184–89.

55. See *Works*, 6, *Tales of War*.

56. Letter 165, to Curtis Brown, 31 December 1896, *Correspondence*. 1:161.

57. Letter 206, 15 February 1896, to the Editor of *The Critic*, *Correspondence*, 1:205.

58. C. B. Ives, "'The Little Regiment' of Stephen Crane at the Battle of Fredericksburg," *Midwest Quarterly* 8 (Spring 1967):247–60.

59. Letter 173, to Nellie Crouse, 6 January 1896, *Correspondence*, 1:171; letter 184, to Nellie Crouse, 12 January 1896, *Correspondence*, 1:180.

60. Henry Fleming makes only one other appearance in Crane's fiction, in the Whilomville story "Lynx-Hunting" (7:138–43).

61. Clark Griffith, "Stephen Crane and the Ironic Last Word," *Philological Quarterly* 47 (January 1968):83–91.

62. Willa Cather, "When I Knew Stephen Crane," *Library* 1 (23 June 1900):17–18. Reprinted in *Prairie Schooner* 23 (Fall 1949):231–36.

63. Letter 416, To Paul Revere Reynolds, 3 November 1898, *Correspondence*, 2:387.

64. One example appeared in a Maine newspaper, the Lewiston *Journal*, and the *New York Tribune* (18 May 1897); quoted in Stallman, *Biography*, 552.

> I have seen a battle.
> I find it is very like what
> I wrote up before.
> I congratulate myself that
> I ever saw a battle.
> I am pleased with the sound of war.

65. Bill Christophersen, "Stephen Crane's 'The Upturned Face' as Expressionist Fiction," *Arizona Quarterly* 38 (Summer 1982):147–61.

66. Although Henry Fleming, in *The Red Badge*, "had been to touch the great death," the phrase may be ironical.

67. Hermann Bahr, "Expressionism," in *Paths to the Present: Aspects of European Thought from Romanticism to Existentialism*, ed. Eugen Weber (New York: Dodd, Mead & Co., 1960).

68. Eugen Weber, introduction to "Expressionism," in *Paths to the Present*, 210.

69. Joseph Conrad to Edward Garnett, 5 December 1897, in *Stephen Crane: Letters*, ed. R. W. Stallman and Lillian B. Gilkes (New York: New York University Press, 1960), 154.

70. Gullason, *Stephen Crane's Career*, 485.

71. Stallman, *Biography*, 368.

Part 2

THE WRITER

Introduction

Stephen Crane's letters are the most complete and, with the possible exception of Herbert P. Williams's interview, the *only* accurate record of his beliefs about life and literature. Williams's interview, reprinted here, cannot be taken entirely as an intimate and reliable account of Crane's views. In the first place, Williams seems more interested in presenting to the public an author more fascinating in his private life than in his work. And second, Crane was seldom completely open with the public.

The recently published *Correspondence of Stephen Crane*, edited by Stanley Wertheim and Paul Sorrentino, provides for the first time an accurate reproduction of Crane's letters. The letters, while "they clarify his attitudes toward literature and the creative process,"[1] must also be looked at carefully. Often, when Crane seems to be at his most unguarded, he is writing to a woman he is trying to impress.

In the letters, excerpts from which are reprinted here, a somewhat different picture of Crane appears from that painted by Thomas Beer in his biography, *Stephen Crane, A Study in American Letters*, and others written over the last century. Crane, it now seems, was even more paradoxical and intriguing than he formerly appeared to have been. He was not Beer's moral paragon walking down the more squalid alleys of life and remaining unsullied. The letters make it clear that, as Wertheim and Sorrentino say, Crane was "alternately shy and self-deprecatory, egocentric and generous, irresponsible and contentious, ingenuous and cynical, ethical and dishonest, rebellious and overly concerned about his reputation."[2]

Interview

*Herbert P. Williams**

A few days ago I called on the author of *The Red Badge of Courage*. When in New York Stephen Crane lives alone in an enormous room at the top of a house near the heart of the city, in the shopping district. The furniture of the room is curiously typical of the man: a tinted wall is relieved at intervals by war trophies and by impressionistic landscapes. The latter might have been painted in any state in the Union: the feeling for color is what you observe; the locality is nothing worthy of remark. The small bookshelf contains batches of gray manuscript and potential literature in the form of stationery. One of the two chairs stands between the window and a writing table at which a club might dine. An ink-bottle, a pen and a pad of paper occupy dots in the vast green expanse. A sofa stretches itself near the window and tries to fill space. No crowded comfort is here—no luxury or ornament—no literature, classic or periodical; nothing but the man and his mind.

During our long talk Mr. Crane proved himself frank, open, natural and completely devoid of affectation. It was the simplicity of the man who "sees things flat." He knows his mind without being self-conscious. He is hampered by nothing, the traditions of the past—the sensationalism and the subjectivity of the present he neither imitates nor criticises. He merely writes what he pleases, that is, what seems to him true; you are privileged to like it; he is your good friend if you don't. It has been said that he describes everything in terms of color; perhaps he would call his position "red independence." After five minutes in his company you will see colors everywhere, even if you did not see them before.

"Why, no," he said, in answer to a question, "I do not find that short stories are utterly different in character from other fiction. It seems to me that short stories are the easiest things we write."

Three years ago, when Mr. Crane had just attained his majority, he

*Reprinted from *Illustrated American* 20 (18 July 1896):xx, 126. Williams was a reporter for the Boston *Herald* and an acquaintance of Crane.

wrote a story of war. He had never seen a battle, of course, and he does not know how he came to choose a war theme. Perhaps it is in the blood; his ancestors were soldiers; Mr. Crane himself, though a small man, made a reputation at Rochester University for successfully resisting attempts at browbeating on the part of the captain of a visiting team; he rejoices in a fight (vide *Maggie*); and he says himself that he gained his knowledge of the sensations of his hero from the football field and elsewhere.

His method, he told me, is to get away by himself and think over things. "Then comes a longing for you don't know what; sorrow, too, and heart-hunger." He mixes it all up. Then he begins to write. The first chapter is immaterial; but, once written, it determines the rest of the book. He grinds it out, chapter by chapter, never knowing the end, but forcing himself to follow "that fearful logical conclusion"; writing what his knowledge of human nature tells him would be the inescapable outcome of those characters placed in those circumstances.

Loving color, he early learned to note it in everything. He learned landscape more than surveying while in college. His observation, cultivated on natural objects, served him well in cities. He knows human nature very well in many of its moods; but of the artificial life of society he knows and cares to know nothing. His manners show it. He has reverted to the unconventional. If he cared to make an impression I suppose he would adopt those formalities which many people consider essential to good breeding. It would be a failure.

But we are getting away from the writer. Here we find an artist who will not play for applause. Mr. Crane has too much good sense, too deep a regard for what he sees, too much determination to describe things clearly, no matter what the medium, to care overmuch for the reader's praise.

"Oh, of course," he said, "I should be glad if everybody, Canadians, Feejees, Hottentots, wild men of Borneo, would buy *The Red Badge*—four copies of it—but they won't; so what's the use of thinking of the reader? If what you write is worthy, somebody will find it out some time. Meanwhile that is not one of the problems that interests me." It is Mr. Crane's contention that any one can describe any sensation if he uses his experience, because suggestion creates so many sensations. "Didn't you ever see through whole years of friendship in the face of a man you met on the street?" But in spite of a vivid imagination that can conjure up almost anything, he does not think to trust the imagination of any one who reads. He puts everything so plainly that you can't help understanding it as he meant it.

"Trust their imaginations? Why, they haven't got any! They are used to having everything detailed for them. Our imaginations are defunct for lack of use, like our noses. So whether I say a thing or suggest it, I try to put it in the most forcible way."

Singular declaration, this, for a man whose books appeal chiefly to men of powerful imagination.

He usually draws his pictures in four sentences like thumb-nail strokes. He has never tried to paint, which he says is fortunate because it would not have been a success. It is fortunate for another reason. Verestschagin has painted the most wonderful pictures of war ever seen. How do his pictures compare with Crane's? Chiefly in three ways:

Verestschagin has lived everything that he has ever painted; his works are highly finished—complete in every detail; and he points a moral. On the other hand Mr. Crane wrote *The Red Badge* from pure power of the imagination to conjure up scenes and sensations: his descriptions tell parts of the landscape and suggest the rest, and he merely states a problem in its barrenness, relying for effect on truth and vividness.

Something in Verestschagin's "All Quiet at Shipka," and in his picture showing the Czar comfortably seated on a knoll while 18,000 Russians are being slaughtered before the redoubts opposite, is a rebuke to existing conditions. Tolstoi, too, writes with an obvious purpose. These three men are alike in this: they see things in their nakedness. It is curious to note that Verestschagin and Crane both have that feeling for the right *kind* of the right color (the right quality of sunlight, for instance). Mr. Crane is not inferior to either Russian in point of truth; but while he has accentuated the individual, Tolstoi and Verestschagin continually preach the insignificance of the unit.

Selected Letters
Letter 31, to Lily Brandon Munroe*

. . . To speak, to tell you of my success, dear, is rather more difficult. My career has been more of a battle than a journey. You know, when I left you, I renounced the clever school in literature. It seemed to me that there must be something more in life than to sit and cudgel one's brains for clever and witty expedients. So I developed all alone a little creed of art which I thought was a good one. Later I discovered that my creed was identical with the one of Howells and Garland and in this way I became involved in the beautiful war between those who say that art is man's substitute for nature and we are the most success-ful in art when we approach the nearest to nature and truth, and those who say—well, I don't know what they say. They don't, they can't say much but they fight villainously and keep Garland and I out of the big magazines. Howells, of course, is too powerful for them.

If I had kept to my clever Rudyard-Kipling style, the road might have been shorter but, ah, it wouldn't be the true road. The two years of fighting have been well-spent. And now I am almost at the end of it. This winter fixes me firmly. We have proved too formidable for them, confound them. . . .

I am doomed, I suppose, to a lonely existence of futile dreams. It has made me better, it has widened my comprehension of people and my sympathy with whatever they endure. And to it I owe whatever I have achieved and the hope of the future. In truth, this change in my life should prove of some value to me, for, ye gods, I have paid a price for it.

*March–April 1894. *Correspondence*, 1:63–64. Crane and Munroe met at Asbury Park in 1892. Wertheim and Sorrentino assert (pp. 55–56) on good evidence that she and Crane were in love, but that she was too mature to leave her unhappy marriage, even for a poor young man.

The Writer

Letter 44, to Copeland and Day*

Messrs. Copeland and Day:—

Dear sirs:—We disagree on a multitude of points. In the first place I should absolutely refuse to have my poems printed without many of those which you just as absolutely mark "No." It seems to me that you cut all the ethical sense out of the book. All the anarchy, perhaps. It is the anarchy which I particularly insist upon. From the poems which you keep you could produce what might be termed a "nice little volume of verse by Stephen Crane" but for me there would be no satisfaction. The ones which refer to God, I believe you condemn altogether. I am obliged to have them in when my book is printed. There are some which I believe unworthy of print. These I herewith enclose. As for the others, I cannot give them up—in the book.

Letter 73, to the Reverend Thomas Dixon*

It is inevitable that this book [*Maggie, A Girl of the Streets*] will greatly shock you, but continue, pray, with great courage to the end, for it tries to show that environment is a tremendous thing in this world, and often shapes lives regardlessly. If one could prove that theory, one would make room in Heaven for all sorts of souls (notably an occasional street girl) who are not confidently expected to be there by many excellent people.

Letter 78, to John Northern Hilliard*

. . . I did little work at school, but confined my abilities, such as they were, to the diamond. Not that I disliked books, but the cut-and-dried curriculum of the college did not appeal to me. Humanity was a much more interesting study. When I ought to have been at recitations I was

*9 September 1894, *Correspondence*, 1:73–74. Copeland and Day brought out Crane's book of poetry, *The Black Riders*.

*January 1895, *Correspondence*, 1:96. The Reverend Thomas Dixon was one of many preachers crying out for reform in the Bowery and one of several to whom Crane sent an inscribed copy of *Maggie*.

*February 1895, *Correspondence*, 1:99. Crane met Hilliard in 1892 when both were reporters in New York City.

studying faces on the streets, and when I ought to have been studying my next day's lessons I was watching the trains roll in and out of the Central Station. So, you see, I had, first of all, to recover from college. I had to build up, so to speak. And my chiefest desire was to write plainly and unmistakably, so that all men (and some women) might read and understand.

Letter 90, to Copeland and Day*

. . . I have considerable work that is not in the hands of publishers. My favorites are eight little grotesque tales of the woods which I wrote when I was clever. The trouble is that they only sum 10000 words and I can make no more. . . .

Letter 128, to Willis Brooks Hawkins*

. . . I have always believed the western people to be much truer than the eastern people. We in the east are overcome a good deal by a detestable superficial culture which I think is the real barbarism. Culture in it's true sense, I take it, is a comprehension of the man at one's shoulder. It has nothing to do with an adoration for effete jugs and old kettles. This latter is merely an amusement and we live for amusement in the east. Damn the east! I fell in love with the straight out-and-out, sometimes-hideous, often-braggart westerners because I thought them to be the truer men and, by the living piper, we will see in the next fifty years what the west will do. They are serious, those fellows. When they are born they take one big gulp of wind and then they live.

Of course, the east thinks them ridiculous. When they come to congress they display a child-like honesty which makes the old east laugh. And yet—

Garland will wring every westerner by the hand and hail him as a frank honest man. I wont. No, sir. But what I contend for is the atmosphere of the west which really is frank and honest and is bound to make eleven honest men for one pessimistic thief. More glory be with them.

*June (?) 1895, *Correspondence*, 1:111.

*A longtime friend of Crane, Hawkins often helped Crane out of financial and other difficulties.

Letter 166, to Nellie Crouse

. . . The lives of some people are one long apology. Mine was, once, but not now. I go through the world unexplained, I suppose. Perhaps this letter may look like an incomparable insolence. Who knows. Script is an infernally bad vehicle for thoughts. I know that, at least.

Letter 170, to Elbert Hubbard

My dear Haich: I read your "No Enemy" today. I always find that I better appreciate what books are to us when I wait for the moment to come when I want a book and want it badly. This afternoon I read "No Enemy" at one sitting. I like it. Your manipulation of the life in Indiana and Illinois is out of sight. There are swift character sketches all through it that strike me as being immense. However, I sympathize with the clergyman in Chapter I. He stated his case rather badly but he was better than Hilliard. Hilliard proved in the rest of the book that he was not what he indirectly said he was in Chapter I. Hilliard is a bird. Yet in Chapter I he was a chump. Your flowers on the water— good god, that is magnificent. A thing that I felt in the roots of my hair. Hell and blazes, but I do envy you that paragraph.

The book strengthened me and uplifted me. It is a peach.
*2 January 1896, *Correspondence*, 1:168–69.

Letter 173, to Nellie Crouse*

. . . I am sending you by this mail a newspaper clipping of "A Grey Sleeve." It is not in any sense a good story and the intolerable pictures make it worse. . . .

*31 December 1895, *Correspondence*, 1:163.

*2 January 1896, *Correspondence*, 1:168–69. Among the literati of his day, Hubbard was editor of the *Philistine* and wrote several books. He engaged Crane for the famous Philistine Banquet.

*6 January 1896, *Correspondence*, 1:171.

Letter 175, to Willis Brooks Hawkins

. . . I am writing a story—"The Little Regiment" for McClure. It is awfully hard. I have invented the sum of my invention in regard to war and this story keeps me in internal despair. However I am coming on with it very comfortably after all. . . .

Letter 184, to Nellie Crouse

. . . For my own part, I am minded to die in my thirty-fifth year. I think that is all I care to stand. I dont like to make wise remarks on the aspect of life but I will say that it doesn't strike me as particularly worth the trouble. The final wall of the wise man's thought however is Human Kindness of course. If the road of disappointment, grief, pessimism, is followed far enough, it will arrive there. Pessimism itself is only a little, little way, and moreover it is ridiculously cheap. The cynical mind is an uneducated thing. Therefore do I strive to be as kind and as just as may be to those about me and in my meagre success at it, I find the solitary pleasure of life.

It is good of you to like "A Grey Sleeve." Of course, they are a pair of idiots. But yet there is something charming in their childish faith in each other. That is all I intended to say. . . .

There is only one person in the world who knows less than the average reader. He is the average reviewer. I would already have been a literary corpse, had I ever paid the slightest attention to the reviewers. . . .

Letter 186, to Nellie Crouse

. . . The story "One Dash—Horses," which I sent you celebrates in a measure my affection for a little horse I owned in Mexico. . . .

I am, too, very tired. So you think I am successful? Well I dont know. Most people consider me successful. At least, they seem to so think. But upon my soul I have lost all appetite for victory, as victory is defined by the mob. I will be glad if I can feel on my death-bed that my

*7 January 1896, *Correspondence*, 1:175.

*12 January 1896, *Correspondence*, 1:180, 181.

*26 January 1896, *Correspondence*, 1:185, 186, 187.

life has been just and kind according to my ability and that every particle of my little ridiculous stock of eloquence and wisdom has been applied for the benefit of my kind. From this moment to that deathbed may be a short time or a long one but at any rate it means a life of labor and sorrow. I do not confront it blithely. I confront it with desperate resolution. There is not even much hope in my attitude. I do not even expect to do good. But I expect to make a sincere, desperate, lonely battle to remain true to my conception of my life and the way it should be lived, and if this plan accomplish anything, it shall be accomplished. It is not a fine prospect. I only speak of it to people in whose opinions I have faith. No woman has heard it until now.

When I speak of a battle I do not mean want, and those similar spectres. I mean myself and the inherent indolence and cowardice which is the lot of all men. . . .

I got an armful of letters from people who declared that The Black Riders was—etc, etc,—and then for the first time in my life I began to be afraid, afraid that I would grow content with myself, afraid that willy-nilly I would be satisfied with the little, little things I have done. For the first time I saw the majestic forces which are arrayed against man's true success—not the world—and the world is silly, changeable, any of it's decisions can be reversed—but man's own colossal impulses more strong than chains, and I perceived that the fight was not going to be with the world but with myself. I had fought the world and had not bended nor moved an inch but this other battle—it is to last on up through the years to my grave and only on that day am I to know if the word Victory will look well upon lips of mine. . . .

Letter 197, to John Northern Hilliard*

The one thing that deeply pleases me in my literary life—brief and inglorious as it is—is the fact that men of sense believe me to be sincere. . . . Personally I am aware that my work does not amount to a string of dried beans—I always calmly admit it. But I also know that I do the best that is in me, without regard to cheers or damnation. When I was the mark for every humorist in the country I went ahead, and now, when I am the mark for only 50 per cent of the humorists of the country, I go ahead, for I understand that a man is born into the world with his own pair of eyes and he is not at all responsible for his quality

*January (?) 1896, *Correspondence*, 1:195, 196.

of personal honesty. To keep close to my honesty is my supreme ambition. There is a sublime egotism in talking of honesty. I, however, do not say that I am honest. I merely say that I am as nearly honest as a weak mental machinery will allow. This aim in life struck me as being the only thing worth while. A man is sure to fail at it, but there is something in the failure.

Letter 200, to Nellie Crouse*

. . . Of course I am admittedly a savage. I have been known as docile from time to time but only under great social pressure. I am by inclination a wild shaggy barbarian. . . .

Letter 204, to Nellie Crouse*

. . . For my part, I like the man who dresses correctly and does the right thing invariably but, oh, he must be more than that, a great deal more. But so seldom is he anymore than correctly-dressed, and correctly-speeched, that when I see a man of that kind I usually put him down as a kind of an idiot. Still, as I have said, there are exceptions. There are men of very social habits who nevertheless know how to stand steady when they see cocked revolvers and death comes down and sits on the back of a chair and waits. . . .

I swear by the real aristocrat. The man whose forefathers were men of courage, sympathy and wisdom, is usually one who will stand the strain whatever it may be. He is like a thorough-bred horse. His nerves may be high and he will do a lot of jumping often but in the crises he settles down and becomes the most reliable and enduring of created things.

For the hordes who hang upon the out-skirts of good society and chant 143 masses per day to the social gods and think because they have money they are well-bred—for such people I have a scorn which is very deep and very intense. These people think that polite life is something which is to be studied, a very peculiar science, of which knowledge is only gained by long practice whereas what is called "form" is merely a collection of the most rational and just of laws which

*5 February 1896, *Correspondence*, 1:197.

*11 February 1896, *Correspondence*, 1:201, 202, 203.

any properly-born person understands from his cradle. In Hartwood I have a great chance to study the new-rich. The Hartwood Club-house is only three miles away and there are some of the new rich in it. May the Lord deliver me from having social aspirations.

I can stand the society man, if he dont interfere with me; I always think the society girl charming but the type that I cant endure is the society matron. Of course there are many exceptions but some I have seen struck me afar off with the peculiar iron-like quality of their thick-headedness and the wild exuberance of their vanity. . . .

I detest dogma. . . .

I hope it will be plain that I strongly admire the social god even if I do despise many of his worshippers. . . .

I get about two letters a day from people who have high literary aims and everywhere I go I seem to meet five or six. They strike me as about the worst and most penetrating kind of bore I know. . . .

Tolstoy's aim is, I suppose—I believe—to make himself good. It is an incomparably quixotic task for any man to undertake. He will not succeed; but he will even succeed more than he can ever himself know, and so at his nearest point to success he will be proportionately blind. This is the pay of this kind of greatness.

Letter 209, to Nellie Crouse*

. . . Dear me, how much am I getting to admire graveyards—the calm unfretting unhopeing end of things—serene absence of passion—oblivious to sin—ignorant of the accursed golden hopes that flame at night and make a man run his legs off and then in the daylight of experience turn out to be ingenious traps for the imagination. If there is a joy of living I cant find it. The future? The future is blue with obligations—new trials—conflicts. It was a rare old wine the gods brewed for mortals. Flagons of despair—

Letter 225, to the Editor of The Youth's Companion*

. . . This lieutenant is an actual person. . . .

---

*1 March 1896, *Correspondence*, 1:207, 208.

*March 1896, *Correspondence*, 1:221. Refers to "An Episode of War."

Letter 236, to The Book Buyer*

I have never been in a battle, of course, and I believe that I got my sense of the rage of conflict on the football field.

Letter 240, to the Editor of
Demorest's Family Magazine*

I have heard a great deal about genius lately, but genius is a very vague word; and as far as I am concerned I do not think it has been rightly used. Whatever success I have had has been the result simply of imagination coupled with great application and concentration. It has been a theory of mine ever since I began to write, which was eight years ago, when I was sixteen, that the most artistic and the most enduring literature was that which reflected life accurately. Therefore I have tried to observe closely, and to set down what I have seen in the simplest and most concise way. I have been very careful not to let any theories or pet ideas of my own be seen in my writing. Preaching is fatal to art in literature. I try to give my readers a slice out of life; and if there is any moral or lesson in it I do not point it out. I let the reader find it for himself. As Emerson said, "There should be a long logic beneath the story, but it should be kept carefully out of sight."

Before "The Red Badge of Courage" was published I often found it difficult to make both ends meet. The book was written during this period. It was an effort born of pain, and I believe that this was beneficial to it as a piece of literature. It seems a pity that this should be so,—that art should be a child of suffering; and yet such seems to be the case. Of course there are fine writers who have good incomes and live comfortably and contentedly; but if the conditions of their lives were harder, I believe that their work would be better. . . . Now that I have reached the goal for which I have been working ever since I began to write, I suppose I ought to be contented; but I am not. I was happier in the old days when I was always dreaming of the thing I have now attained. I am disappointed with success. Like many things we strive for, it proves when obtained to be an empty and a fleeting joy.

*April 1896, *Correspondence*, 1:228.

*Late April–early May 1896, *Correspondence*, 1:230, 231.

The Writer

Letter 241, to J. Herbert Welch*

. . . I was always very fond of literature, though. I remember when I was eight years old I became very much interested in a child character called, I think, Little Goodie Brighteyes, and I wrote a story then which I called after this fascinating little person. When I was about sixteen I began to write for the New York newspapers, doing correspondence from Asbury Park and other places. Then I began to write special articles and short stories for the Sunday papers and one of the literary syndicates, reading a great deal in the meantime and gradually acquiring a style. I decided that the nearer a writer gets to life the greater he becomes as an artist, and most of my prose writings have been toward the goal partially described by that misunderstood and abused word, realism. Tolstoi is the writer I admire most of all. . . .

Letter 275, to Belle Walker*

Dear Miss Walker: I think the motif of the story is properly strong. "You will never hold the cross toward me." That, I think is very effective. One thing I must say at once: Take the diamond out of that man's shirt immediately. Dont let him live another day with a diamond in his front. You declare him to be very swell and yet you allow him to wear a diamond as if he were a saloon proprietor or owned a prosperous livery stable. It is of the utmost importance that you remove the diamond at once for our fin de siecle editors have keen eyes for that sort of a mistake.

Frankly I do not consider your sketch to be very good but even if you do me the honor to value my opinion, this need not discourage you for I can remember when I wrote just as badly as you do now. Furthermore there are many men, far out superiors who once wrote just as badly as I do today and no doubt as badly as you.

*Late April–early May 1896, *Correspondence*, 1:232.

*8 September 1896, *Correspondence*, 1:253. Belle Walker remains unidentified, but she must have been an aspiring writer who asked Crane's opinion of her work.

Letter 276, to Paul Revere Reynolds*

I leave you a story of something over 5000 words, which I like you to sell if you can. It is one of the best stories that I have done and the lowest price that I could take for it would be $350. . . . [Refers to "A Man and Some Others."]

Letter 334, to Paul Revere Reynolds*

. . . "The Bride Comes to Yellow Sky" is a daisy and don't let them talk funny about it. . . .

Letter 338, to Joseph Conrad*

My dear Conrad: My first feat has been to lose your note and so I am obliged to send this through Heineman. I have read the proof sheets which you so kindly sent me and the book is simply great. The simple treatment of the death of Waite is too good, too terrible. I wanted to forget it at once. It caught me very hard. I felt ill over that red thread lining from the corner of the man's mouth to his chin. It was frightful with the weight of a real and present death. By such small means does the real writer suddenly flash out in the sky above those who are always doing rather well. . . . [Refers to Conrad's *The Nigger of the "Narcissus."*]

Letter 352, to John Northern Hilliard*

. . . I know what the psychologists say, that a fellow can't comprehend a condition that he has never experienced, and I argued that many times with the Professor. Of course, I have never been in a battle, but I believe that I got my sense of the rage of conflict on the football field, or else fighting is a hereditary instinct, and I wrote in-

---

*9 September 1896. *Correspondence*, 1:254. Reynolds was Crane's American literary agent.

*October 1897, *Correspondence*, 1:305.

*11 November 1897, *Correspondence*, 1:310. Conrad was Crane's best literary friend.

*1897 (?), *Correspondence*, 1:322.

tuitively; for the Cranes were a family of fighters in the old days, and in the Revolution every member did his duty. But be that as it may, I endeavored to express myself in the simplest and most concise way. If I failed, the fault is not mine. I have been very careful not to let any theories or pet ideas of my own creep into my work. Preaching is fatal to art in literature. I try to give to readers a slice out of life; and if there is any moral or lesson in it, I do not try to point it out. I let the reader find it for himself. The result is more satisfactory to both the reader and myself. As Emerson said, "There should be a long logic beneath the story, but it should be kept carefully out of sight." Before "The Red Badge of Courage" was published, I found it difficult to make both ends meet. The book was written during this period. It was an effort born of pain, and I believe that it was beneficial to it as a piece of literature. It seems a pity that this should be so—that art should be a child of suffering; and yet such seems to be the case. Of course there are fine writers who have good incomes and live comfortably and contentedly; but if the conditions of their lives were harder, I believe that their work would be better. Bret Harte is an example. He has not done any work in recent years to compare with those early California sketches. Personally, I like my little book of poems, "The Black Riders," better than I do "The Red Badge of Courage." The reason is, I suppose, that the former is the more ambitious effort. In it I aim to give my ideas of life as a whole, so far as I know it, and the latter is a mere episode, or rather an amplification. Now that I have reached the goal, I suppose that I ought to be contented; but I am not. I was happier in the old days when I was always dreaming of the thing I have now attained. I am disappointed with success, and I am tired of abuse. Over here [England], happily, they don't treat you as if you were a dog, but give every one an honest measure of praise or blame. There are no disgusting personalities.

Letter 416, to Paul Revere Reynolds*

. . . The name of the story is "The Price of the Harness" because it *is* the price of the harness, the price the men paid for wearing the military harness, Uncle Sam's military harness; and they paid blood, hunger and fever. . . .

---

*3 November 1898, *Correspondence*, 2:387.

Letter 608, to Thomas Hutchinson (?)*

I am not carnivorous about living writers. I have not read any of the books that you ask me to criticize except that of Mr. Howells, and it has disappointed me. My tastes? I do not know of any living author whose works I have wholly read. I like what I know of Anatole France, Henry James, George Moore, and several others. I deeply admire some short stories by Mr. Bierce, Mr. Kipling and Mr. White. Mr. Hardy, since you especially inquire about his work, impresses me as a gigantic writer who "overtreats" his subjects. I do not care for the long novels of Mr. Clemens, for the same reason. Four hundred pages of humour is a little bit too much for me. My judgment in the case is not worth burning straw, but I give it as portentously as if kingdoms toppled while awaiting it under anxious skies.

Letter 728, to an Unknown Recipient*

I can not see why people hate "ugliness" in art. Ugliness is just a matter of treatment. The scene of Hamlet and his mother and the death of old Polonius behind the curtain is ugly, if you heard it in a police court. Hamlet treats his mother like a drunken carter and his words when he has killed Polonius are disgusting. But who cares? You are hearing something fine in the theater and the fine quality of it gives you a kind of quick sympathy with Mr. Shakespeare. . . .

Letter 744, to an Unknown Recipient*

What, though, does the man mean by disinterested contemplation? It won't wash. If you care enough about a thing to study it, you are interested and have stopped being disinterested. That's so, is it not? Well, Q.E.D. It clamours in my skull that there is no such thing as disinterested contemplation except that empty as a beerpail look that a babe turns on you and shrivels you to grass with. Does anybody know how a child thinks? The horrible thing about a kid is that it makes no

*1899, *Correspondence*, 2:566.

*Spring 1891, *Correspondence*, 2:662, appendix A.

*1895, *Correspondence*, 2:670, appendix A.

excuses, none at all. They are much like breakers on a beach. They do something and that is all there is in it.

Letter 746, to Catherine Harris*

. . . I do not think that much can be done with the Bowery as long as the . . . [illegible] . . . are in their present state of conceit. A person who thinks himself superior to the rest of us because he has no job and no pride and no clean clothes is as badly conceited as Lillian Russell. In a story of mine called "An Experiment in Misery" I tried to make plain that the root of Bowery life is a sort of cowardice. Perhaps I mean a lack of ambition or to willingly be knocked flat and accept the licking. The missions for children are another thing and if you will have Mr. Rockefeller give me a hundred street cars and some money I will load all the babes off to some pink world where cows can lick their noses and they will never see their families any more. My good friend Edward Townsend—have you read his "Daughter of the Tenements"?— has another opinion of the Bowery and it is certain to be better than mine. I had no other purpose in writing "Maggie" than to show people to people as they seem to me. If that be evil, make the most of it.

Letter 739, to an Unknown Recipient*

If you hear that I have been hanged by the neck till dead on the highest hill of Orange County you may as well know that it was for killing a man who is really a pug—No, by the legs of Jehovah! I will not insult any dog by comparing this damned woman to it. There is a feminine mule up here who has roused all the bloodthirst in me and I don't know where it will end. She has no more brain than a pig and all she does is to sit in her kitchen and grunt. But every when she grunts something dies howling. It may be a girl's reputation or a political party or the Baptist Church but it stops in its tracks and dies. Sunday I took a 16 yr. old child out driving in a buggy. Monday this mule addresses me in front of the barber's and says, "You was drivin' Frances out yesterday" and grunted. At once all present knew that Frances and I

*12 November 1896, *Correspondence*, 2:671, appendix A.

*Late November 1894, *Correspondence*, 2:666, 667, appendix A.

should be hanged on twin gallows for red sins. No man is strong enough to attack this mummy because she is a nice woman. She looks like a dried bean and she has no sense, but she is a nice woman. Right now she is aiming all her artillery at Cornelia's new hat. I have been deprived by heaven of any knowledge of hats but it seems to be a very kindly hat with some blue flowers on one side and a ribbon on the other. But we rustle in terror because this maggot goes to and fro grunting about it. If this woman lived in Hester Street some son or brother of a hat would go bulging up to her and say, "Ah, wot deh hell!" and she would have no teeth any more, right there. She is just like those hunks of women who squat on porches of hotels in summer and wherever their eye lights there blood rises. Now, my friend, there is a big joke in all this. This lady in her righteousness is just the grave of a stale lust and every boy in town knows it. She accepted ruin at the hands of a farmer when we were all 10 or 11. But she is a nice woman and all her views of all things belong on the tables of Moses. No man has power to contradict her. We are all cowards anyhow. . . .

Letter 750, to an Unknown Recipient*

This girl in Zola is a real streetwalker. I mean, she does not fool around making excuses for her career. You must pardon me if I cannot agree that every painted woman on the streets of New York was brought there by some evil man. Nana, in the story, is honest. . . . Zola is a sincere writer but—is he much good? He hangs one thing to another and his story goes along but I find him pretty tiresome.

Letter 760, to an Unknown Recipient*

[I like] a great many passages in the work of Tolstoy, so many that Tolstoy ranks as the supreme living writer of our time to me. But I confess that the conclusions of some of his novels, and the lectures he sticks in, leave me feeling that he regards his genius as the means to an end. I happen to be a preacher's son, but that heredity does not preclude—in me—a liking for sermons unmixed with other material.

*Early 1897, *Correspondence*, 2:673, appendix A.

*1897, *Correspondence*, 2:677, appendix A.

No, that sentence doesn't mean anything, does it? I mean that I like my art straight.

Letter 784, to an Unknown Recipient*

I am sending you Mr. James's new book. Please be very careful of it, as you see that the inscription makes it a personal affair. Hope that you find it interesting. I got horribly tired half through and just reeled along through the rest. You will like some of it a lot. But I do not think that his girl in the cage is exactly an underclass clerk in love with a "man about town." Women think more directly than he lets this girl think. But notice the writing in the fourth and fifth chapters when he has really got started. . . .

Letter 785, to an Unknown Recipient*

No thanks. If the Whilomville stories seem like Little Lord Fauntleroy to you you are demented and I know that you are joking, besides. See here, my friend, no kid except a sick little girl would like Lord Fauntleroy unless to look at Birch's pictures for it. The pictures are all right.

Letter 788, to an Unknown Recipient*

I should say that Mr. [H. G.] Wells will write better and better when he sticks to characters altogether and does not so much concern himself with narrative. I may be wrong but it seems to me that he has a genius for writing of underclass people more honestly than Charles Dickens. . . . I will bet all my marbles and my best top hat that Walter Besant is forgotten in twenty years. . . . Every one tells me that Mr. Stevenson was a fine fellow but nothing on earth could move me to change my belief that most of his work was insincere.

---

*1899, *Correspondence*, 2:688, appendix A. "Mr. James's new book" is *In the Cage*.

*1899, *Correspondence*, 2:688, appendix A.

*1899, *Correspondence*, 2:690, 691, appendix A.

Letter 790, to an Unknown Recipient*

We tell kids that heaven is just across the gaping grave and all that bosh and then we scare them to glue with flowers and white sheets and hymns. We ought to be crucified for it! . . . I have forgotten nothing about this, not a damned iota, not a shred.

*[?] *Correspondence*, 2:691, appendix A.

Part 3

THE CRITICS

Introduction

The following critical appraisals represent only a small part of the excellent criticism available on Crane's work. While none but Nagel's has been anthologized before, each deserves to have been, for each represents not only a particular "angle," in James Dickey's words, of Crane's art, but each presents it well. *Deliverance,* Dickey's own novelistic "rush into the red universe," and whose characters correspond closely to those of "The Open Boat," would alone qualify him to speak on Crane, but he seems also to be secure in the same tradition of American writers as is Crane—the tradition of the "active life" that includes Twain and Hemingway as well. He conveys here in very few words the sense of intellectual excitement derived from reading Crane, the sense that Crane writes about things of ultimate importance. Thomas Gullason, a prolific critic of Crane, was the first to write at length on the idea that the short stories in Crane's collections are linked thematically. James Nagel, in *Stephen Crane and Literary Impressionism,* collects and synthesizes the many scattered critical appraisals of Crane's Impressionism and adds his own considerable insights. H. G. Wells, whom Rebecca West called the most intelligent man of his generation of literati, presents a contemporary response to Crane's work that is as insightful today as it was when he wrote it in 1900. Milne Holton's *Cylinder of Vision* has never received the praise it deserves. His thorough, often brilliant, analysis of Crane's fiction is constantly being reinvented by critics, but seldom so well as Holton himself presents it, especially in the passage on "Death and the Child." J. C. Levenson's introductions to several volumes of the *Works,* especially volume 7, *Tales of Whilomville,* have also been overlooked. He does much to unravel the well-known Gordian knot of the dates of composition of some of Crane's stories. At the same time, he provides analyses filled with intelligence and common sense.

Stephen Crane

James Dickey*

He had the angle. The Crane slant of vision came into a scene or onto an action or a personality with terrible ironic penetration, and it came from a direction and a distance that no one could have suspected was there, much less have predicted. He came from nowhere, and is with us, bringing his peculiar and unforgettable kind of detached animism, sometimes frightening, sometimes ludicrous, the objects and peoples of the world all being seen as comments on or complements of each other, and none of them safe from this. War and poverty are Crane's best themes, and the needless suffering of animals. The cosmos is filled with the most stupefying fear about which, inexplicably, there is also something funny. After reading him, we ponder the possibility that we had better use more caution before we "rush out into the red universe any more."

From Stephen Crane as Short-Story Writer

Thomas A. Gullason*

Although literary historians and critics usually applaud a writer's achievements in the short story, they rarely allot much discussion to them; they give more emphasis and time to the writer's plays, poetry, or novels. Even now in the 1970s, there is little appreciation of the aesthetics of the short story. In addition, short-story collections are looked upon as ephemera, odds and ends left over from novels, or trial

*From *Stephen Crane in Transition: Centenary Essays,* ed. Joseph Katz. © 1972 by Northern Illinois University Press, De Kalb, Illinois. Reprinted by permission of the publisher.

*From *Stephen Crane's Career: Perspectives and Evaluations,* ed. Thomas A. Gullason (New York: New York University Press, 1972), 407–9. Reprinted by permission of the publisher.

runs for novels. All this places Crane at a distinct disadvantage, since he showed his skill best when he wrote short stories.

Both Edward Garnett and H. L. Mencken, among others, respected Crane mainly as a short-story writer; while they increased understanding of Crane's art and brilliance, they admitted to his "limitations." To Garnett, Crane was a master of the short story and of impressionism, but his art was "strictly limited." He was the "interpreter of the surfaces of life," and a student of the "fragmentary." Crane, concluded Garnett, should never "have essayed the form of the novel." Mencken respected Crane's "superlative" talent in "handling isolated situations," but his method "was grossly ill-adapted to the novel." To later critics and readers, Garnett and Mencken present weak arguments for the "narrow" scope of Crane's art.

There are other, more specific reasons why Stephen Crane was not taken seriously as a short-story writer. During his brief literary career—roughly 1892 to 1900—Crane wrote more than a hundred short stories and fictional sketches. This made him "prolific," a term often associated with carelessness. In his letters from England, Crane indicated that he was anxious about his financial debts; he also said that he wanted to write short stories because he could do them faster, and to postpone beginning a novel because it would take too much time. All of this suggested that he was not deeply concerned about the quality of his writing. In addition to his reporting, many of his short stories appeared in newspapers, so that people connected Crane with journalism more than with fiction. Moreover, so much discussion and focus have been placed on *Maggie* and *The Red Badge* that anything else was given secondary stress. Nor could anyone's career as a short-story writer end so tragically. When Cora Crane put together *Last Words* (1902), a posthumous potpourri of Crane's early and late fiction and journalism, it proved to many that Crane did not mature, and probably never was much of an artist.

But between some of his earliest work in *The Sullivan County Sketches* (1892) and his late stories, like "The Squire's Madness," Stephen Crane wrote some major American short stories. Attention has centered for decades on four of them: "The Open Boat," "The Blue Hotel," "The Bride Comes to Yellow Sky," and "The Monster." Significantly, each of these stories has recently been read in new ways that suggest a greater understanding and respect for Crane's artistry and vision. For years, "The Bride Comes to Yellow Sky" was read as a satiric comedy, or as a hilarious parody; lately, a few critics have challenged these readings by pointing to Crane's fundamental seriousness in the western tale. One of the charges leveled against "The Monster" was that it lacked unity. Recent studies show that the story is indeed skillfully organized; this new insight into its unity elucidates and extends the thematic meanings and nuances of the work. Each new study of "The Open Boat" and "The Blue Hotel" opens up new complexities, new proofs of Crane's skill as artist and thinker. If Crane could never be identified as a tragic artist because of his supposedly naturalistic and deterministic bias, he is now being appreciated as a tragedian. The next step is to recognize in his short stories the rich blend of tragedy and comedy, namely tragi-comedy.

In his best stories, Crane was the supremely balanced writer, able to rise above nagging problems with cleverness, boyish posturings, and superficial reflections on reality. The newspaper "feature," such as "An Experiment in Misery," taught Crane the value of seriousness and deeper insight into reality; it also proved to him the need for art and imagination in order to get beyond the topical newspaper report. There was a classic wedding in his great stories between theme and form, realism and romance, and imagination and experience.

Stephen Crane's talent as a short-story writer can be respected more if critics and readers view some of his collections as novels-of-short-stories. . . . Crane's first real collection of short stories was *The Little Regiment and Other Episodes of the American Civil War*. By comparing and contrasting people, places, attitudes, tones, and themes, Crane's work in *The Little Regiment* is much more than "miniature" leftovers from *The Red Badge*. It makes up, as the subtitle to the collection suggests, a series of individual episodes or scenes from the Civil War, which give the work as a whole a unity and experience similar to that of the novel form.

The eight short stories in the American edition of *The Open Boat and Other Tales of Adventure* also accumulate and display the variety and largeness of the novel world through thematic and artistic parallels and contrasts in the stories, though some of the efforts, like "Flanagan and His Short Filibustering Adventure" and "One Dash—Horses" are by themselves lesser works. Note, for example, how "Flanagan" echoes "The Open Boat." The design of *The Open Boat* was somewhat altered in the English edition, to which Crane added a group of New York pieces, *Midnight Sketches*. When viewed together, these New York sketches are even more valuable artistically and thematically, for they make up a novel of city scenes. Even *Whilomville Stories* becomes more valuable, for by adding up the thirteen separate glimpses into the life of the child, the reader gains a remarkable and panoramic view into the child's everyday world of drama, fun, and pain.

By "collecting" his stories and thereby viewing art and reality from differing perspectives, beginning with *The Sullivan County Sketches*, Stephen Crane gradually learned to distill more into later individual stories. His best works, like "The Blue Hotel," are deeper, richer, and more profound; they have more originality, power, art, and meaning than the earlier tales and sketches.

Critics are just starting [in 1972] to probe the genre of the short story; they are showing more respect for the "episodic" and the "fragmentary" form, which in the past they had considered as poorly structured and containing little to say. . . . [I hope that] in the future, critics and readers will find even more life and value in Stephen Crane's short stories.

From Stephen Crane and the Narrative Methods of Impressionism

*James Nagel**

The fundamental method of Impressionism is the presentation of sensation so as to create the effect of immediate sensory experience, a device which places the reader at the same epistemological position in the scene as the character involved. The qualifying variable in this method is the determination of the human intelligence which receives the sensations, a matter not operative in Impressionistic painting and music because those forms proceed on the assumption that it is the artist or composer who does the perceiving. But fiction involves a formulating center of intelligence, a narrator who, in Impressionism, projects not what *he* perceives but what is apprehended and understood by one or more of the characters. The effect is a distancing from the

*From *Studies in the Novel* 10 (Spring 1978): 76–85. © 1978 by Northern Texas State University. Reprinted by permission of the publisher.

author, a sensory objectivity which requires extraordinary skill in estab-
lishing verisimilitude. . . .

The limitation of narrative data in fiction to the narrator's projection
of the mind of a character is central to Impressionism, as is the suggestion that the perceiving intelligence is a qualification of the definition of reality, that perceptions are relative and potentially unreliable,
that interpretations of reality are forever tentative, and that other minds
may perceive the same phenomenon in other terms. One extension of
this logic leads to narrative modulations of shifting perspectives, of
multiple, sometimes reduplicative presentations of scenes in narrative
parallax; another would lead to narrative irony, to the concentration not
only on sensory data but on the way it is perceived at either the apprehensional or comprehensional level. For example, in the opening paragraph of "The Bride Comes to Yellow Sky" the narrator can assert, as
the train whirls westward carrying Jack Potter and his bride, that "the
plains of Texas were pouring eastward. Vast flats of green grass, dull-
hued space of mesquite and cactus, little groups of frame houses,
woods of light and tender trees, all were sweeping over the horizon, a
precipice." . . .

The theoretical logic of Impressionism thus tends toward variations
of limited narrative perspectives. First-person narration is attractive
here, but problematic: it contains the virtue of spatial immediacy but
the enigma of temporal dislocation. In nearly all of its expressions it
implies a dual time scheme, a time of telling subsequent to the time
of action; the narrator thus renders memory rather than sensory experience. As a basically Impressionistic writer, Crane had difficulty with
this mode and used it infrequently and in one of his finest works. His
few first-person works, however, reveal fascinating manipulations of
perspective which bring them into greater conformity with Impressionistic concepts. "A Tale of Mere Chance," for example, is a dramatic
monologue which presents the ironic revelations of a murderer telling
his story after his capture. What the story reveals is that his judgment
of himself is inconsistent with the very facts he presents: he has shot
a man point-blank and without warning yet attempts to maintain his
view of himself as a "delicate and sensitive person." The story portrays
his pervasive guilt and the interpretive aberrations of his mind, as is
especially evident in his surrealistic personification of inanimate ob-

jects. According to *his* version of it, when he attempted to escape the scene of the murder, the chair moved to block the door; the clock speaks to betray his alibi; his blood-stained coat clings to him; the floor tiles, stained by blood, pursue him, relentlessly "shrieking" his guilt. The story is first person, but more suggestive of Impressionistic distortion than of traditional uses of the method. Another example is "An Illusion in 'Red and White,'" in which the narrator can only speculate about what happened and in which the children, eyewitnesses to the murder of their mother, delude themselves completely by the end of the story. The result of Crane's handling of first person is to introduce unreliability and irony as important modifiers of the plot, a device Ford Madox Ford used with success in *The Good Soldier.*

Another traditional narrative device theoretically problematic for Impressionism is third-person omniscient, since, by the logic of its own assumptions, it is not dependent upon the empirical data of the fiction for its information. Only a few of Crane's works are truly consistent with the terms of omniscience, and these are among his least impressive works. . . .

If first-person narration is temporally awkward for Impressionism, and omniscience philosophically discordant, its natural expression is third-person limited, the mode Crane almost consistently used, although with numerous variations. Crane's method is basically focused on the sensory and associational experience of the central character. His style is thus understandably laden with verbs of perception. . . .

But an even more emphatic example of Crane's Impressionistic strategies is the presentation of sensory data under extraordinary circumstances of restriction. He relates one such moment in his "London Impressions" in describing the experiences of a carriage ride: "Each man sat in his own little cylinder of vision, so to speak. It was not so small as a sentry-box, nor so large as a circus-tent, but the walls were opaque, and what was passing beyond the dimensions of his cylinder no man knew." The "cylinder of vision" concept, which Milne Holton used for the title of his impressive book, is a useful metaphor for the implicit human condition in all of Crane's work and a suggestive indicator of his manner of narration. Perhaps the most dramatic brief demonstration of this method is in a little-studied story entitled "Three Miraculous Soldiers," in which the point of view is essentially restricted to the mind of its female protagonist, Mary Hickson, who gains much of her information, especially at the most suspenseful moments, by peering through a knothole into a dimly lit barn.

The opening of the story reveals Crane's typical method of progressive intensification: the first paragraph describes Mary and the room she is in from the outside perspective of a third-person narrator: "The girl was in the front room on the second floor, peering through the blinds." The point of view is outside of Mary and yet is not omniscient: the narrator must speculate that the two clay figures on the mantel are "probably" a shepherd and shepherdess. Beyond introducing a characteristic uncertainty, the opening paragraph also defines Mary's initial angle of vision which then controls the second paragraph: "from between the slats of the blinds she had a view of the road as it wended across the meadow to the woods and again where it reappeared crossing the hill, a half mile away." Now there are no comments beyond Mary's knowledge; implied, but not stated, is the suggestion that she is deeply concerned with the activity on the road, of which she can see only part. By the third paragraph the narrative perspective is limited to Mary's mind and her sensory information: "Mary's eyes were fastened upon the little streak of road that appeared on the distant hill. Her face was flushed with excitement and the hand which stretched in a strained pose on the sill trembled because of the nervous shaking of the wrist. The pines whisked their green needles with a soft hissing sound against the house."

The story progresses on these limited terms. When Mary speaks to someone downstairs, "a voice" answers. Not until further dialogue establishes the identity of the voice does the narrator clarify that it is that of the mother. This method is similar to that in *The Red Badge*, in which speakers are identified only by descriptive epithets until personal names have been mentioned in dialogue. When the soldiers first appear on the road, they do so at a distance, a fact rendered Impressionistically: "Upon the yellow streak of road that lay across the hillside there now was a handful of black dots—horsemen." It is indicative of Crane's method of presenting apprehension before cognition that he does not say that "soldiers" appeared in the distance. Mary's eyes perceive "black dots" which are then interpreted as horsemen, the next level of analysis, and finally as soldiers, as opposed to other categories of horsemen.

To Mary's point of view is added another, one equally limited: "Rushing to the window, the mother scanned for an instant the road on the hill." The mother responds with fright, apparently from what the soldiers might do, but it is clear that they are still at some distance, for in a moment "the black dots vanished into the wood." Soon the girl can hear the "quick, dull trample of horses." When they appear, the forest suddenly "disclosing" them in their blue uniforms, the fictional situation is further clarified: this is a house in the South; Mary and her family are loyal Confederates; the Union army is advancing. The perspective briefly shifts to that of the officer in charge of the group, revealing his lack of interest in the house and its inhabitants. His insouciance becomes significant when set against the counteranalysis of his motives by the mother, who is convinced that the ruthless Yankees are about to take advantage of two defenseless women. Emotional preoccupation, in subjective Impressionistic terms, serves to distort the interpretation of sensory data. As a result, the women hear the crackling of the fire in the kitchen as the movement of soldiers: "These sounds were sinister." Apprehensive data has now become mingled with interpretive distortions on the secondary level of Impressionistic information. The first section of the story ends when Mary goes to the barn to relieve her fears that her horse has been stolen and discovers three Confederate soldiers hiding from the Union advance. Again, the narrative emphasis is on restriction: at first "the girl could not see into the barn because of the heavy shadows." In a moment, when her eyes adjust to the light, her perception is of "three men in gray" sitting on the floor. That the men are Confederate soldiers in hiding is left to the reader to induce.

The next section of the story retains its restriction on the point of view to Mary's mind and what she is able to see. As she speaks to the soldiers, seeking information about her father, and as a large group of Union cavalry ride into the yard, the emphasis is on how little Mary can see and understand the events. The trees and a henhouse obscure her view of the arriving troops; she has to leave the barn to get a better look at them; once in the house, she moves about from window to window, each revealing only a partial view of the scene. No clarifying information is introduced here from any source other than Mary's mind. By the end of the section she has hidden the three men in the feed box in the barn and the Union soldiers have decided to imprison a captured Confederate there as well, not knowing of the presence of the others.

The next section becomes increasingly vivid in its projection of sensory details as the scene becomes obscure and limited. As it begins to grow dark, Mary, back in the house peering out the window, perceives the muted colors before her: "Tones of grey came upon the fields and the shadows were of lead." The fires in the encampment shine more brilliantly, "becoming spots of crimson color in the dark grove." As the light fades even further, visual data becomes more indistinct: trees become black "streaks of ink"; groups of soldiers become "blue clouds" about the fire. A lantern hung in the barn distorts the view: "Its rays made the form of the sentry seem gigantic." Auditory sensation, understandably, is not affected: the whinny of the horses, the "hum" of distant conversation, the calls of the sentries are all received clearly. That all of this is Impressionistic in broad terms is further suggested by Mary's assessment of the scene in the orchard, with campfires glowing in the darkness, as one "like a great painting, all in reds upon a black cloth." Finally, in the ultimate restriction of narrative data, Mary, stealing to the rear of the barn to confirm the safety of her compatriots in the feed box, puts her eye to a knothole. Much of the rest of the story is rendered from this perspective.

There is a tense scene when a Union officer opens the feed box and finds nothing but grain. Having no access to data beyond her own experience, Mary is startled and mystified. Incapable of accounting for the disappearance of the three men, Mary's mind perceives the feed box as a mysterious object "like some dark magician's trap." Through the knothole, the Union soldiers cast "monstrous wavering shadows" in the lantern light; the roof of the barn becomes an "inscrutable blackness." Her mind becomes incapable of interpreting sensory data reliably: hearing sounds at her feet, she first "imagines" that she sees human hands protruding from under the barn; then she realizes that they are, in fact, hands; then she sees a man crawling out. Despite the dramatic circumstances, there is more stress on Mary's problems of perception and interpretation than on suspenseful activity. The three Confederates escape from the barn only to learn that their captain is still being held within. They decide to attempt to rescue him.

As the soldiers return to the barn, Mary resumes her vigil at the knothole, and what is revealed about the ensuing action is limited to what she can perceive from this vantage point. When she first looks about the area, "she searched with her eyes, trying to detect some moving thing, but she could see nothing." She thinks she can see a figure moving in the darkness, but she is not sure: "At one time she saw it plainly and at other times it vanished, because her fixture of gaze caused her occasionally to greatly tangle and blur those peculiar shadows and faint lights. At last, however, she perceived a human head." Her other perceptions are equally difficult. The sounds of activity which come to her are incomprehensible: she can interpret them only in general terms as a "tumult," as the "scramble and scamper of feet," as voices yelling "incoherent" words. As the sentry moves into her vision, however, and as her sense of his danger from the creeping men within the barn grows, she focuses sharply on his "brown hair," "clear eyes," and on the ring on his finger signifying marriage. When the men finally leap upon the sentry, Mary's passive reception of details ends and she screams, inadvertently creating a diversion which allows the four Confederates to escape. The story ends with the Union lieutenant reflecting on Mary's concern for the sentry, an indication that despite war some elements of universal human compassion survive.

"Three Miraculous Soldiers" is no more a real story of war than is *The Red Badge*. The story is perhaps Crane's best use of suspense in the narrative line, but even the suspense is a product of the narrative method. Told from an omniscient point of view, there could have been little suspenseful interest. The story is artistically and ideologically a study in the limitations of sensory data, rendered, with some contrasts from other limited viewpoints, from the mind of Mary Hickson under conditions of extraordinary restriction. Although there are other elements of interest (the depiction of war from the point of view of a southern woman; melodramatic plot developments; a concern for the father off at war), the fundamental themes and methods of this story are Impressionistic. Indeed, the lengthy scenes told on the basis of what Mary can perceive through the knothole constitute one of the most remarkably limited narrative perspectives in American literature.

A few of Crane's other methods of narration, all coordinated with central Impressionistic implications, deserve comment. One such device is the "camera eye" technique used in the fight scene in "The Blue Hotel" when the perspective becomes that of the Easterner: "during this pause, the Easterner's mind, like a film, took lasting impressions of three men—the iron-nerved master of the ceremony; the Swede, pale, motionless, terrible; and Johnnie, serene yet ferocious, brutish yet heroic." Limited to the vision of the Easterner, a small man, fraught with anxiety, peering into a snowstorm, the narrator can record only fragmentary glimpses: "For a time the encounter in the darkness was such a perplexity of flying arms that it presented no more detail than would a swiftly-revolving wheel. Occasionally a face, as if illuminated by a flash of light, would shine out, ghastly and marked with pink spots." This scene is similar to one in "A Man and Some Others" in which another Easterner observes a gunfight at night between Bill and a bank of Mexicans attempting to run him off the range: "The lightning action of the next few moments was of the fabric of dreams to the stranger. . . . And so the fight, and his part in it, had to the stranger only the quality of a picture half drawn."

An especially noteworthy narrative device used by Crane is "parallax," the device of narrating from more than one point of view, usually two or more limited perspectives, occasionally limited views set off against an omniscient narrator. Crane used this method throughout his life, from "Uncle Jake and the Bell-Handle," a story written when he was only fourteen, and in which the rustic Uncle Jake's perspective is comically juxtaposed to that of the worldly-wise urban clerks, to similar devices in "The Bride Comes to Yellow Sky" and "The Open Boat," to perhaps his most notable implementation of the method in "Death and the Child." In this story Peza's view of war as an heroic struggle is counterpointed by the view of the child, who sees it as an extension of his game of shepherding. The contrasting points of view in such works reinforce the notion of relativity, that phenomenological perception is as important in understanding reality as the external objects themselves. And it is historically important to remember that Crane's use of parallax is antecedent to Ernest Hemingway's use of it in "The Short Happy Life of Francis Macomber" and William Faulkner's more sophisticated implementation in *The Sound and the Fury* and *As I Lay Dying*.

To make a simple statement about an extremely intricate matter, Stephen Crane's narrative methods are a good deal more complex than has generally been assumed, especially by those readers who would simply identify the narrators of his works as Crane himself. His narrative methods, almost without exception, portray a world which is "ephemeral, evanescent, constantly shifting its meaning and hence continually defying precise definition," a description Rodney O. Rogers uses to describe both Crane's works and French Impressionistic painting. Narrative restrictions, limitations of sensory data, distorted interpretations of information, modulations among differing points of view, these are Crane's methods of presentation. As a more complete analysis of Crane's works would reveal, these narrative strategies are related to his episodic plots, his sensory images, his epistemological themes involving perception and realization. As a totality, Crane's works suggest a human situation in which the individual is almost inconsequential in the universal matrix and yet is a dramatic modifier of all of reality he can ever know, a situation in which any view of circumstances is limited, philosophically tentative, and certain to be challenged by contrasting views. It is an unsettling yet aesthetically satisfying conception, one remarkably modern and existential for the 1890s, one basic to what has been called Crane's "vision," and one central to the fundamental implications of literary Impressionism.

From Stephen Crane from an English Standpoint
*H. G. Wells**

The untimely death at thirty of Stephen Crane robs English literature of an interesting and significant figure, and the little world of those who write, of a stout friend and a pleasant comrade. For a year and more he had been ailing. The bitter hardships of his Cuban expedition had set its mark upon mind and body alike, and the slow darkling of the shadow upon him must have been evident to all who were not blinded by their confidence in what he was yet to do. Altogether, I knew Crane for less than a year, and I saw him for the last time hardly more than seven weeks ago. He was then in a hotel at Dover, lying still and comfortably wrapped about, before an open window and the calm and spacious sea. If you would figure him as I saw him, you must think of him as a face of a type very typically American, long and spare, with very straight hair and straight features and long, quiet hands and hollow eyes, moving slowly, smiling and speaking slowly, with that deliberate New Jersey manner he had, and lapsing from speech again into a quiet contemplation of his ancient enemy. For it was the sea that had taken his strength, the same sea that now shone, level waters beyond level waters, with here and there a minute, shining ship, warm and tranquil beneath the tranquil evening sky. Yet I felt scarcely a sus-

*From the *North American Review*, 171 (August 1900): 233–42. Reprinted by permission of the University of Northern Iowa.

picion then that this was a last meeting. One might have seen it all, perhaps. He was thin and gaunt and wasted, too weak for more than a remembered jest and a greeting and good wishes. It did not seem to me in any way credible that he would reach his refuge in the Black Forest only to die at the journey's end. It will be a long time yet before I can fully realize that he is no longer a contemporary of mine; that the last I saw of him was, indeed, final and complete.

Though my personal acquaintance with Crane was so soon truncated, I have followed his work for all the four years it has been known in England. I have always been proud, and now I am glad, that, however obscurely, I also was in the first chorus of welcome that met his coming. It is, perhaps, no great distinction for me; he was abundantly praised; but, at least, I was early and willing to praise him when I was wont to be youthfully jealous of my praises. . . .

"Death and the Child" . . . is considered by very many of Crane's admirers as absolutely his best. I have carefully re-read it in deference to opinions I am bound to respect, but I still find it inferior to the earlier work. The generalized application is, to my taste, a little too evidently underlined; there is just that touch of insistence that prevails so painfully at times in Victor Hugo's work, as of a writer not sure of his reader, not happy in his reader and seeking to drive his implication (of which also he is not quite sure) home. The child is not a natural child; there is no happy touch to make it personally alive; it is THE CHILD, something unfalteringly big; a large, pink, generalized thing, I cannot help but see it, after the fashion of a Vatican cherub. The fugitive runs panting to where, all innocent of the battle about it, it plays; and he falls down breathless to be asked, "Are you a man?" One sees the intention clearly enough; but in the later story it seems to me there is a new ingredient that is absent from the earlier stories, an ingredient imposed on Crane's natural genius from without—a concession to the demands of a criticism it had been wiser, if less modest, in him to disregard—criticism that missed this quality of generalization and demanded it, even though it had to be artificially and deliberately introduced.

The Open Boat is to my mind, beyond all question, the crown of all his work. It has all the stark power of the earlier stories, with a new element of restraint; the color is as full and strong as ever, fuller and stronger, indeed; but those chromatic splashes that at times deafen and confuse in *The Red Badge*, those images that astonish rather than enlighten, are disciplined and controlled. "That and 'Flanagan,'" he told me, with a philosophical laugh, "was all I got out of Cuba." I cannot say whether they were worth the price, but I am convinced that these two things are as immortal as any work of any living man. And the way *The Open Boat* begins, no stress, plain—even a little gray and flattish. . . .

From that beginning, the story mounts and mounts over the waves, wave frothing after wave, each wave a threat, and the men toil and toil and toil again; by insensible degrees the day lights the waves to green and olive, and the foam grows dazzling. Then as the long day draws out, they come toward the land. . . .

The Open Boat gives its title to a volume containing, in addition to that and "Flanagan" certain short pieces. One of these others, at least, is also to my mind a perfect thing, "The Wise Men." It tells of the race between two bartenders in the city of Mexico, and I cannot imagine how it could possibly have been better told. And in this volume, too, is that other masterpiece—the one I deny—"Death and the Child."

Now I do not know how Crane took the reception of this book, for he was not the man to babble of his wrongs; but I cannot conceive how it could have been anything but a grave disappointment to him. To use the silly phrase of the literary shopman, "the vogue of the short story" was already over; rubbish, pure rubbish, provided only it was lengthy, had resumed its former precedence again in the reviews, in the publishers' advertisements and on the library and book-sellers' counters. The book was taken as a trivial by-product, its author was exhorted to abandon this production of "brilliant fragments"—anything less than fifty thousand words is a fragment to the writer of literary columns— and to make that "sustained effort," that architectural undertaking, that alone impresses the commercial mind. Of course, the man who can call *The Open Boat* a brilliant fragment would reproach Rodin for not completing the edifice his brilliant fragments of statuary are presumably intended to adorn, and would sigh, with the late Mr. Ruskin for the day when Mr. Whistler would "finish" his pictures. Moreover, he was strongly advised—just as they have advised Mr. Kipling—to embark upon a novel. And from other quarters, where a finer wisdom might have been displayed, he learned that the things he had written were not "short stories" at all; they were "sketches" perhaps, "anecdotes"—just as they call Mr. Kipling's short stories "anecdotes"; and it was insinuated that for him also the true, the ineffable "short story" was beyond his reach. I think it is indisputable that the quality of this reception, which a more self-satisfied or less sensitive man than Crane might have ignored, did react very unfavorably upon his work. They put him out of conceit with these brief intense efforts in which his peculiar strength was displayed. . . .

He began stark—I find all through this brief notice I have been repeating that in a dozen disguises, "freedom from tradition," "absolute directness" and the like—as though he came into the world of letters without ever a predecessor. In style, in method and in all that is distinctively *not* found in his books, he is sharply defined, the expression in literary art of certain enormous repudiations. Was ever a man before who wrote of battles so abundantly as he has done, and never had a word, never a word from first to last, of the purpose and justification of the war? And of the God of Battles, no more than the battered name: "Hully Gee?"—the lingering trace of the Deity! . . .

It is as if the racial thought and tradition had been razed from his mind and its site ploughed and salted. He is more than himself in this; he is the first expression of the opening mind of a new period, or, at least, the early emphatic phase of a new initiative—beginning, as a growing mind must needs begin, with the record of impressions, a record of a vigor and intensity beyond all precedent.

On "Death and The Child"
Milne Holton

. . . In "Death and the Child" Crane imaginatively came to terms with the understanding which, as I have said, must precede that of "the mental attitude of the men." He came to terms with the meaning of war for himself, and with the implications of the search for that meaning. . . .

From *Cylinder of Vision: The Fiction and Journalistic Writing of Stephen Crane.* © 1972 by Louisiana State University Press. Reprinted by permission of the publisher.

Milne Holton

At the beginning of the story Peza is presented as an acutely sensitive and highly educated young man, come to the battlefield to apprehend for himself the reality of war. The isolation implicit to such a man at such a task is established at the outset, when Peza is set in opposition to the natural flow of humanity, which is in flight from war. "The peasants who are streaming down the mountain trail had, in their sharp terror, evidently lost their ability to count. The cattle and the huge round bundles seemed to suffice to the minds of the crowd if there were now two in each case where there had been three. This brown stream poured on with a constant wastage of goods and beasts. . . . It was as if fear was a river. . . . It was a freshet that might sear the face of the tall quiet mountain." In contrast to the apprehension of these peasants, inexact and fearful as it is, there is another way of seeing, an apprehensional state in which the senses are acute and objective and the emotions are disengaged. And the narrating voice of the story ironically and suddenly imposes this alternative by, as it were, turning around and, presumably with its back to these fleeing peasants, describing in quite a different style what these peasants do not see. Now the reader is presented, not with a "stream" but with another body of water. "The blue bay, with its pointed ships, and the white town lay below them, distant, flat, serene. There was upon this vista a peace that a bird knows when, high in the air, it surveys the world, a great, calm thing rolling noiselessly toward the end of the mystery." . . .

There is here a radical—an absurd—dichotomy between the human creature and the natural universe, a dichotomy which, if it is to be bridged, must be bridged by means of an individual human understanding. Peza, who like Crane has formulated the purpose of apprehending and perhaps even interpreting, stands somewhere between these two possibilities, in the position in which that individual human understanding is possible. Peza is an intellectual, and the objectivity of his apprehension separates him from the fleeing peasants just as distance separates him from the warring soldiers. His purpose is to diminish that distance without losing the objectivity of his apprehension. Crane's purpose is to test whether such an undertaking is possible.

Peza's movement toward confrontation involves the shortening of emotional as well as physical distance. Yet, as he moves to the top of the first hill in the first stage of his progress to the crest of the mountain and to his confrontation with the actuality of war itself; he has as his Virgil in this Dantesque journey an officer whose experience, restraint,

129

and limits of vision contrast sharply with Peza's innocence, enthusiasm, and ambition for full understanding. The officer is "quiet and confident, respecting fate, fearing only opinion," while Peza's observation soon turns to sympathy, and his desire to apprehend soon becomes a search for actual participation. The officer, whose dust-covered uniform contrasts with Peza's freshly new clothing, attempts to restrain the correspondent, even to warn at one point that "there is no time for this" as Peza's sympathy overflows. Soon, however, Peza has left his companion behind and gone on from the artillery positions on the plain to a mountain howitzer position and finally to the infantry and their line of battle atop the mountain.

Peza has, of course, set out to see war, and throughout his progress up the mountain everything is presented in the language of seeing. The reader's attention is constantly called to characters' eyes—to the "flash of eyes" of the lieutenant, to the fact that Peza's "eyes glistened." Battle wounds are seen in ironic contrast to the illustrated instructions printed on the cloth provided to bind them. Shifts in perspective are meticulously recorded, as Peza occasionally pauses in his ascent to observe the panorama of battle.

As Peza moves up the mountain, however, "the full lens of his mind" is exposed to a number of obstacles to vision. One, of course, is the simple satiation of sight. He recognizes that the experience of seeing the battle is similar to that of the visual satiation one sometimes encounters after too long in a picture gallery, and, as he lights a passing soldier's cigarette, he recognizes in the soldier's eyes the same satiation. And the experience of battle brings with it another limitation, a limitation not unlike that of the lieutenant—or of the peasants fleeing down the mountain. For Peza also soon becomes aware that "his whole vision was focussed upon his own chance." Another obstacle is, of course, the artificial order which participants always impose upon the natural chaos of battle; this is perhaps best symbolized by the rituals of military conduct, which are often described in Crane's story. When the lieutenant, Peza's guide, leaves the correspondent, "they bowed punctiliously, staring at each other with civil eyes," and, when Peza then climbs farther up the mountain, he comes upon an artillery unit whose conduct is extremely formalized and mannerly. Come to "look this phenomenon [war] in the face," Peza continually finds his apprehension blocked by the formal manners of professional soldiers.

The obscuring rituals are lessened as Peza climbs to the even higher infantry position. But now these obstacles are replaced by another, by something within Peza himself—his own animal fear. At the top of the mountain he finally has his opportunity to confront and to apprehend the actual hand-to-hand fighting. As he approaches, he first behaves in a courageous, even reckless manner. He sees an attack forming and runs along the crest of the mountain to meet it ("it was incredible recklessness thus to call to himself the stare of thousands of hateful eyes"). When he finally arrives at the Greek infantry position, he is given an opportunity to join in the fight. But before he begins to participate, he must confront directly that necessary ingredient—indeed that essence—of war which Crane himself had confronted in the body of the Greek soldier. Peza is told to equip himself by removing the bandoleer from a corpse, but when he turns to this ultimate confrontation, this touching of death itself, he falters. He is frozen with fear, is unable even to remove the blanket which covers the corpse. A soldier must retrieve the needed equipment for him.

Peza masters his fear for a moment and dons the bandoleer, but then an experience—more intense even than sight—seizes Peza's imagination, and, in one of Crane's most grotesquely rendered passages, the reader sees Peza completely immobilized by an audio-tactile fantasy. "Peza, having crossed the long cartridge-belt on his breast, felt that the dead man had flung his two arms around him." . . .

Again the quality of Peza's apprehension is established by contrast with that of his companions, whose experience at that moment, far from being fantastic, is very real, very comradely, and even very gustatory.

All about him were these peasants, with their interested countenances, gibbering of the fight. From time to time a soldier cried out in semi-humorous lamentations descriptive of his thirst. One bearded man sat munching a great bit of hard bread. Fat, greasy, squat, he sat like an idol made of tallow. Peza felt dimly that there was a distinction between this man and a young student who could write sonnets and play the piano quite well. The old blockhead was coolly gnawing at the bread, while he, Peza, was being throttled by a dead man's arms.

He looked behind him, and saw that a head by some chance had been uncovered from the blanket. Two liquid-like eyes were staring into his face. The head was turned a little sideways as if to get a better opportunity for scrutiny. Peza could feel himself blanch; he was being drawn and drawn by these dead men slowly, firmly down as to some mystic chamber under the earth where they could walk, dreadful figures, swollen and blood-marked. He was bidden; they had commanded him; he was going, going, going.

Here the corner of Peza's war experience is turned. Now, failing in the attempt to participate and to objectify, he withdraws from participation and apprehension, away from present actuality and into the isolation of his terrifying private fantasy. As that fantasy—in all its synaesthetic horror—overpowers Peza and obliterates his sense of reality, and as point of view is simultaneously shifted, the narrative voice reports that the correspondent bolts and runs. The final image of the section establishes another isolating fact, another difference between Peza's way of seeing and that of the other men. "The soldier with the bread placed it carefully on the paper beside him as he turned to kneel in the trench."

Crane's conclusion to "Death and the Child," although somewhat clumsily handled, is to my mind not "sentimental," as Stallman and other critics have suggested. Rather, by virtue of its ending, "Death and the Child" becomes profoundly tragic. In the final section, Crane employed a rather innocent and unconditioned point of view, a point of view rather gratuitously and intrusively established earlier in the story, to set the terms of Peza's tragedy. Earlier, Crane had described a child, left behind by its refugee parents and playing on the top of the mountain and within hearing distance of the battle. Now the child is used as a point of view to describe what happened to Peza and to voice a compellingly and dramatically ironic question. . . .

"Are you a man?" . . .

Like Harry of Ernest Hemingway's "The Snows of Kilimanjaro," Peza has come to the top of the mountain. Here he has confronted, in a child's innocent question, the fact of his own dehumanization, the result of the experience he himself had sought. For Peza's sensibility, so acute at the beginning of the story, has been violated precisely because of its responsiveness. Now Peza, fish-like, is hardly more aware than were the animal-like peasants of the story's opening paragraph. . . .

. . . it is Peza's very capacity to apprehend which has defeated and dehumanized him. And, although Crane was to see many more battles and to write of them in his few remaining years, he would describe no more keen sensibilities on his battlefields.

On the Whilomville Tales

*J. C. Levenson**

Stephen Crane's tales of Whilomville range in form from his last great short novel "The Monster" to some of the simplest sketches he ever wrote, just as they range in texture from his uniquely mannered and sometimes apocalyptic high style to prose of the opposite kind, austere and open and plain. But as the stories began to accumulate, Crane saw them as constituting a single group. Although he wanted to bring together the separately published earlier pieces and the series from *Harper's Magazine*, which began to appear in August, 1899, and pre-empted the title *Whilomville Stories*, circumstances of publication forestalled his desire. Yet his instinct in the matter was right. There is a unity to the stories, and it is rightly suggested by the name of the town which provides a common setting to them all. Whilomville, like Thomas Bailey Aldrich's Rivermouth and Mark Twain's St. Petersburg, had its model in the author's actual experience. Port Jervis, New York, where Crane lived from the age of seven until he was twelve, was more truly the scene of his boyhood than any of the several other towns where his father's ministerial calling took him, and as the place of his father's death it marked the closing of one major chapter of boyhood. His brother William settled in Port Jervis and became a successful lawyer there. Another brother, Edmund, whom Stephen chose as guardian after his mother died, moved in the nineties to Hartwood in the hilly and wooded back country some twenty miles from Port Jervis, and eventually he too settled in the town itself. This was the area Stephen Crane thought of as home, the place he was "from." The town provided a resource of stored observation on which he found he could draw almost without limit. It was a place, on the other hand, from which he

*From the introduction to *The University of Virginia Edition of The Works of Stephen Crane*, ed. Fredson Bowers (Charlottesville: University Press of Virginia, 1969–1976). Vol. 7, *Tales of Whilomville*, 1969, xi–xvi. Reprinted by permission of the publisher.

was decidedly cut off. By the time he began using Port Jervis as literary material in the latter part of 1897, he had taken up residence in England; and by 1899, when he was writing the Whilomville series for *Harper's*, he had missed his last chance of going back. The tales in which he created his town of Once-upon-a-time, the ideal American small town of memory and imagination, appeared to be sketches from life, but they were in fact the recollections of an expatriate.

Crane had his reasons for not modeling directly from life. For one thing, he was defensive about his fellow townsmen. After his first taste of English snobbery, he was ready to stand up and declare, "The simple rustic villagers of Port Jervis have as good manners as some of the flower of England's literary set." But he was also defensive *against* his fellow townsmen. When his brother William let him know that "The Monster" had prompted a certain amount of local gossip, Stephen cannily replied, "I suppose that Port Jervis entered my head while I was writing it but I particularly dont wish them to think so because people get very sensitive and I would not scold away freely if I thought the eye of your glorious public was upon me." He had in fact taken care to cover his tracks. . . .

. . . even though Whilomville is important as the setting for the stories, it is not very fully realized as a place. Neither houses nor rooms nor streets nor landscapes are given a specific, independent existence. The local color which editors recommended for giving short tales and sketches a larger coherence is noticeably absent. Port Jervis was, despite Crane's affectionate joking about the "simple rustic villagers," a typical county seat and market center, with a monument to its canal builder as well as its Civil War dead. It was not very active, perhaps, but it was part of the larger world. Crane had an interest in its earlier history, but he did not feel called upon to record a real or fictitious past or any special flavor of local custom or dialect. Indeed, Whilomville is indefinite with respect to time as well as space. Although the presence of children at or near the center of the stories seems to invite the reader's nostalgia, there is no calendar by which the feeling can be measured. There is no sense of an irrevocable past and no concentration on the process of memory recapturing what is lost. There is no sense, either, of a vanishing present. Although the stories are presented as if they have just taken place, the now of the fiction seems to be unchanging. Whilomville exists outside of time, exempt from progress. But when the people, the place, and the historical moment are none of them particularized, the result is realism with a difference. There is still the illusion of actuality, enforced by the immediacy, accuracy, and vividness of Crane's writing, but the traditional categories by which realists had understood their materials are dispensed with.

Crane's representational technique is not the only reason why Whilomville bears the stamp of reality. The town is real, not because it can be photographically verified or rationally located in accordance with common-sense geography or history, but because it existed, as it still exists, in the minds of men. It is the embodiment of the tacit beliefs which Crane shared with his countrymen, real in the sense that it could palpably affect their lives and yet as intangible as any other cultural construct. It is an ideal American society, not faultless by any means, since an ideal—to be believed in—must be believable, but basically humane, equalitarian, and peaceful. It is a middle-class utopia, in which the state has virtually disappeared along with all evidence of public life. Here the concerns of men center in private interest and domestic life. Here, also, the rule of equality provides that even children and their desires and feelings are to be taken seriously. The principles by which this fictive society is organized are real enough for commentators from Tocqueville on to have noticed them at work in the actual America they were observing. Crane offered no ideological scheme by which to explain the way people conducted themselves in their business and public lives, but he did render the utopian ideal by which they seriously wished to organize their common life. And if calling Whilomville a utopia makes it sound "unreal" in this respect, it is important to remember that this model society stands in contrast to the spurious utopia of sentimentalism, in which such social aims are reduced to mere wishfulness and treated as if they explained all behavior.

Thus the dream world of *Little Lord Fauntleroy*, a book which Crane thought "no kid except a sick little girl would like," offered a foil for realism. It set, for popular taste, a standard according to which Thomas Bailey Aldrich and Mark Twain and Stephen Crane all wrote stories of bad boys. Obviously the word *bad*, as the opposite of *too good to live*, left plenty of room for Tom Bailey or Tom Sawyer or Crane's Jimmie Trescott to be fundamentally good. By allowing for mischief and a natural aptitude for minor lying, Crane and the others gave realistic plausibility to materials which sentimental perfectionists habitually falsified. By writing of "bad" boys, they could present a more convincing image of the small town as an unfallen world, a good society with real people in it. By their psychological accuracy they made it seem that such a social order was attainable or, even, attained somewhere not very far away.

In "The Monster," the first of his Whilomville tales, Crane put the town into a fuller context than in any of the later stories. The domestic certitudes are there, but they do not by any means define the boundaries of the presented world. With an accuracy of notation that extended far beyond the children of the tale, he told how Dr. Trescott, firmly set in the established order and prompted only by motives of which his society approved, acted to bring on himself a relentless process of exclusion and alienation. At this level of generalization, one can even say that the story is taken from life: not that the incidents of the story actually occurred, but that Crane analogized from his own experience. Just as he claimed to have learned the emotions of *The Red Badge of Courage* on the football field, he could be said to have learned the emotions of "The Monster" in the events which cut him off from Port Jervis, from New York, and from the United States. What his experience taught was that in order to remain in the comfortable safety of the domestic order, it was not enough to have the prescribed virtues of honesty, good intentions, and a sense of obligation. Even in the realm of imagination, these virtues proved dangerous. Honesty, for example, the main tenet of Howellsian realism, led him early into dark areas which it took Howells many years to reach. The distinctive note of his writing was the perception of a world beyond the accepted order he had been brought up to cherish. His special subjects, war and poverty, were beyond the pale of gentility, but subject matter alone did not account for his alienation. Howells himself proved that the motive of informing the educated public of scenes, situations, and social classes beyond their everyday awareness was by and large compatible with American middle-class values. For Crane, however, seeing "with his own pair of eyes" included something more than careful observation from the proper point of view. A devastating intuition lay behind the skill with which this son of a Methodist minister could render the tabooed world of the urban underclass or the unthinkable chaos of a ruling violence. We went beyond the objectivity of the cool, broadminded reporter and penetrated to a radically different psychological landscape where the moral assumptions of his literate audience did not hold. Those assumptions were in large part his own, and they account for the side of Crane that spoke of cowardice as underlying the Bowery frame of mind. Yet he could also, without moralizing, present the despair of pure wretchedness and the difference that is permanently made by an "experiment in misery." On the one hand, he assumed that the virtues to which he was brought up would stand him well in any circumstance: "The man whose forefathers were men of courage, sympathy and wisdom, is usually one who will stand the strain whatever it may be." On the other hand, though he deplored people who could not learn to live with the impulse to bolt, he attained his great success in *The Red Badge of Courage* by showing how easily one could move into the psychic chaos of fear. His capacity to enter such feelings led to his conceiving a whole otherworld as it might be felt, and in his fiction he presented two categorically different realms of being. He made a radical distinction between the order of the Established and the chaos of the Other Reality. The man who knew both was, in the language of *The Red Badge*, a "veteran," one who was able to experience the chaos and yet eventually resume his place in the ranks. But Crane never let his readers forget that crossing into the otherworld changed a man forever, if he lived. From the beginning he shaped his fiction to the theme of you-can't-go-home-again. . . .

Chronology

1871 1 November: Stephen Crane born in Newark, New Jersey, to the Reverend Jonathan Townley Crane and Mary Helen Peck Crane, as their fourteenth and last child. The Cranes came from old stock; the original American Stephen Crane, in fact, settled in Elizabethtown, New Jersey, in 1665. Another Stephen Crane (1709–80) had been President of the Colonial Assemblies and a New Jersey delegate to the Continental Congress, but he returned home shortly before his fellow delegates signed the Declaration of Independence.

1874–1878 The Reverend Crane serves the Methodist churches in Bloomington and later, in Paterson, New Jersey. Mrs. Crane is active in the Women's Christian Temperance Union, and she and her husband are occasional writers of religious works.

1878 A sickly child, Crane begins schooling in Port Jervis, New York, where the family moved with the Reverend Crane, who serves the Drew Methodist Church. The place where Crane considered himself to be "from," Port Jervis and other rural settings like Hartwood, become the locales for *The Sullivan County Tales and Sketches*, *The Monster and Other Stories*, and *Whilomville Stories*.

1880 16 February: Crane's father dies.

1883 The Crane family moves to Asbury Park, a summer-resort town on the New Jersey coast. Crane's older brother, William, remains in Port Jervis to practice law. During summer, another brother, Townley, runs a news-reporting service in Asbury Park for the *New York Tribune*. This seaside resort probably provides the setting for such early stories as "The Reluctant Voyagers" and "The Pace of Youth."

1884   Agnes Crane, the sibling to whom Crane was closest, dies at twenty-eight of spinal meningitis.

1885–1887   Crane attends Pennington Seminary, a Methodist boarding school once headed by his father. Crane writes (but never publishes) his first story, "Uncle Jake and the Bell Handle."

1888   January: Crane enrolls in Claverack College and Hudson River Institute, Claverack, New York. During the summer Crane begins to write for brother Townley's press bureau, a practice he continues until 1892.

1890   February: Crane's first sketch, "Henry M. Stanley," is published in the Claverack College *Vidette*. Indulges his early love of the military and becomes cadet captain of a student military group. Crane leaves Claverack after two and one-half years, and on 12 September enrolls in the engineering curriculum of Lafayette College. Joins Delta Upsilon fraternity and plays intramural baseball. Having failed his courses, he does not return after Christmas holiday.

1891   9 January: Crane enrolls in Syracuse University. Spends more time playing shortstop and catcher on the varsity baseball team than attending classes; writes for *New York Tribune* and, tradition holds, begins *Maggie*. Publishes his first short story, "The King's Favor," in May issue of the *University Herald*. Summer: meets Hamlin Garland after attending and reporting on Garland's lecture on William Dean Howells; as a stringer for the *New York Tribune*, Crane publishes a hoax called "Great Bugs of Onondaga." Fall: camps with friends in Pike County, Pennsylvania, an experience that contributes to several Sullivan County sketches. Fails to return to Syracuse, and moves to New York City, where he discovers the slums of the Bowery. 7 December: Crane's mother dies.

1892   Many sketches about Asbury Park published, including "A Broken-down Van," which appears to anticipate *Maggie*. Later, an article in the *Tribune*, "Parades and Entertainments," offends both labor and capital interests, and as Whitelaw Reid, the *Tribune's* publisher, is Republican candidate for vice-president, Crane is fired. He settles into a rooming house in Manhattan. Begins to publish regularly such *Sullivan County Tales and Sketches* as "The Last of the Mohicans," "Hunting Wild Hogs," "The Last Panther," "Not Much of a Hero," "Sullivan County Bears," "The Way in Sullivan County," "A Reminiscence of Indian War," "Four Men in a Cave," "The Octopush," "Bear and Panther," "The Ghoul's Accountant," "The Black Dog," "Two Men and a Bear," "Killing His Bear," "A Tent in Agony," and "The Cry of the Huckleberry Pudding."

1893   Crane pays for private printing of *Maggie: A Girl of the Streets*, by "Johnston Smith." It flops. Garland introduces Crane to William Dean Howells. Crane begins *The Red Badge of Courage*. Moves to East 23rd Street.

1894   Writes poetry, *George's Mother*, such stories as "An Experiment in Misery" and "An Experiment in Luxury," and the journalistic piece, "In the Depths of A Coal Mine." An abridged version of *The Red Badge* is published by Bacheller Syndicate newspapers.

1895   Crane falls in love with Nellie Crouse, but she is cautious and does not encourage him. Crane travels in the West and Mexico, reporting for Bacheller. Meets Willa Cather in Nebraska. 11 May: *The Black Riders*, a book of poetry, is published. Summer: with brother Edmund and family at Hartwood, New York, where he writes *The Third Violet*. 5 October: *The Red Badge* published in the United States. November: *The Red Badge* published in England. Crane is famous.

1896   Perhaps has an affair with Amy Leslie, and meets Cora Stewart [Taylor], undoubtedly his last mistress, at her brothel, "Hotel de Dream." Crane writes love letters to both ladies during the same period, but Stewart soon becomes his common-law wife. Leslie and Crane engage in frantic exchange of letters, and she later sues for the return of an $800 loan to him. His relationship with Cora is more stable, but for the rest of Crane's life, she spends more money than he makes. Publishes *George's Mother*,

The Third Violet, many stories and poems, and a somewhat sanitized version of *Maggie*. Crane's first collection of short stories appears as *The Little Regiment and Other Episodes of The Civil War*. After serving as a witness for the defense in the New York City trial of a prostitute, Dora Clark, Crane is driven from the city by gossip and persecution. Travels to Jacksonville, Florida, hoping to go to Cuba to report on the insurrection there.

1897 1 January: Crane embarks on the *Commodore*, a ship running guns to Cuba. 2 January: *Commodore* sinks. 3 January: Crane and three others in a 10-foot dinghy wash ashore near Jacksonville. One man drowns. Crane uses this adventure to write "The Open Boat," which is published in June. April–May: In Greece with Cora ("Imogene Carter") to report the Greco-Turkish War. Goes to England with Stewart ("Mrs. Crane") where they live at Ravensbrook, Oxted, Surrey. Meets Henry James, Harold Frederic, Kate Lyon, William Heinemann, and Joseph Conrad. Crane and Conrad become friends.

1898 25 April: the United States declares war on Spain. Rejected for military service, Crane reports the Spanish-American War for Joseph Pulitzer and, later, for William Randolph Hearst. Acting as a courier, Crane sees much action and writes his best journalism. Ill with a fever, Crane goes to the United States, but returns to Puerto Rico and then Havana, where, heavily in debt, he disappears to write in peace for three months. November: he returns to New York before leaving for England. Several of the great short stories—"The Bride Comes to Yellow Sky," "The Blue Hotel," and "Death and the Child"— are published. *The Open Boat and Other Tales of Adventure* published in April.

1899 Crane returns to England with Cora Stewart, and rents Brede Place, a fourteenth-century manor, from Moreton Frewen, husband of the sister of Lady Randolph Churchill, mother of Winston Churchill. Writes furiously to pay off debts. Produces *War is Kind*, *Active Service*, and another collection of short stories: *The Monster and Other Stories*. Suffering from recurring bouts with fever, and ill with tuberculosis, Crane hemorrhages badly during a Christmas party. He continues, nevertheless, to try to write his way out of debt.

1900 *Whilomville Stories* and *Wounds in the Rain* are published. Cora takes Crane to a sanitorium in Badenweiler, Germany, where he dies on 5 June, aged twenty-eight. His body is returned to the United States where a funeral service is attended by the young Wallace Stevens. Crane is buried in the Evergreen Cemetery in Hillside, New Jersey.

1901 *Great Battles of the World*, a collection of Crane's historical nonfiction, is published. Much of this work was left unfinished at his death, and completed by Kate Frederick, widow of Harold Frederick.

1902 *Last Words*, a collection of miscellaneous and previously unpublished stories and sketches, is published.

1903 *The O'Ruddy: A Romance*, an unfinished novel by Crane, is completed by writer Robert Barr, Crane's friend, and is published.

Bibliography

Primary Sources

Crane, Stephen. *University of Virginia Edition of the Works of Stephen Crane.* Edited by Fredson Bowers. 10 vols. Charlottesville: University Press of Virginia, 1969–1976.

Crane, Stephen. *The Notebook of Stephen Crane.* Edited by Donald J. Greiner and Ellen B. Greiner. Charlottesville: Bibliographical Society of the University of Virginia, 1969.

Crane, Stephen. *The Correspondence of Stephen Crane.* Edited by Stanley Wertheim and Paul Sorrentino. New York: Columbia University Press, 1988.

Secondary Sources

Books

Åhnebrink, Lars. *The Beginnings of Naturalism in American Fiction: A Study of the Works of Hamlin Garland, Stephen Crane, and Frank Norris.* New York: Russell & Russell, 1961.

Bergon, Frank. *Stephen Crane's Artistry.* New York and London: Columbia University Press, 1975.

Berthoff, Werner. *The Ferment of Realism.* New York: Free Press, 1965.

Cady, Edwin H. Introduction to volume 8 of *The University of Virginia Edition of the Works of Stephen Crane.* Edited by Fredson Bowers. 10 Vols. 1969–1976. Charlottesville: University Press of Virginia.

———. *Stephen Crane.* Twayne United States Authors Series 23. New York: Twayne Publishers, Inc., 1962.

Cazamajou, Jean. *Stephen Crane (1871–1900): Écrivai Journaliste.* Études Anglaises 35. Paris: Librairie Didier, 1969.

Colvert, James B. Introductions to volumes 6 and 9 of *The University of Virginia Edition of the Works of Stephen Crane.* Edited by Fredson Bowers. 10 vols. 1969–1976. Charlottesville: University Press of Virginia.

Fried, Michael. *Realism, Writing, Disfiguration: On Thomas Eakins and Stephen Crane.* Chicago: University of Chicago Press, 1987.

Gibson, Donald B. *The Fiction of Stephen Crane.* Carbondale: Southern Illinois University Press, 1968.

Bibliography

Holton, Milne. *Cylinder of Vision: The Fiction and Journalistic Writings of Stephen Crane*. Baton Rouge: Louisiana State University Press, 1972.

Katz, Joseph. *Stephen Crane in the West and Mexico*. Kent, Ohio: Kent State University Press, 1970.

Knapp, Betina L. *Stephen Crane*. New York: Ungar, 1987.

La France, Marsden. *A Reading of Stephen Crane*. London and New York: Oxford University Press, 1971.

Levenson, J. C. Introductions to volumes 5 and 7 of *The University of Virginia Edition of the Works of Stephen Crane*. Edited by Fredson Bowers. 10 volumes. 1969–76. Charlottesville: University Press of Virginia.

Nagel, James. *Stephen Crane and Literary Impressionism*. University Park, Pa.: Pennsylvania State University Press, 1980.

Solomon, Eric. *Stephen Crane: From Parody to Realism*. Cambridge, Mass.: Harvard University Press, 1966.

Wolford, Chester L. *The Anger of Stephen Crane: Fiction and the Epic Tradition*. Lincoln: University of Nebraska Press, 1983.

Articles and Parts of Books

Bender, Bert. "The Nature and Significance of 'Experience' in 'The Open Boat.'" *Journal of Narrative Technique* 9, no. 1 (1979):70–79.

Brennan, Joseph X. "Stephen Crane and the Limits of Irony." *Criticism* 11 (Spring 1969):190–200.

Christophersen, Bill. "Stephen Crane's 'The Upturned Face' as Expressionistic Fiction." *Arizona Quarterly* 38, no. 2 (1982):147–61.

Colvert, James B. Introduction to *Great Short Works of Stephen Crane*. New York: Harper & Row, 1979.

Deamer, Robert Glen. "Remarks on the Western Stance of Stephen Crane." *Western American Literature* 15 (Summer 1980):122–31.

Elison, Ralph. "Stephen Crane and the Mainstream of American Fiction." In *Shadow and Act*, 60–76. New York: Random House, 1953.

Ellis, James. "The Game of High-Five in 'The Blue Hotel.'" *American Literature* 49 (November 1977):440–42.

Gerstenberger, Donna. "'The Open Boat': Additional Perspective." *Modern Fiction Studies* 17 (Winter 1971–72):558.

Gleckner, Robert F. "Stephen Crane and the Wonder of Man's Conceit." *Modern Fiction Studies* 5 (Autumn 1959):271–81.

Griffith, Clark. "Stephen Crane and the Ironic Last Word." *Philological Quarterly* 47 (January 1968):83–91.

Gullason, Thomas A. "Stephen Crane as Short-Story Writer: An Introduction." In *Stephen Crane's Career: Perspectives and Evaluations*, edited by Thomas A. Gullason, 407–9. New York: New York University Press, 1972.

Hagemann, E. R. "'Sadder Than the End': Another look at 'The Open

Boat.'" In *Stephen Crane: Centenary Essays*, edited by Joseph Katz, 66–85. DeKalb: Northern Illinois University Press, 1972.

Johnson, Clarence O. "Mr. Binks Read Emerson: Stephen Crane and Emerson's 'Nature.'" *American Literary Realism, 1870–1910* 15, no. 1 (Spring 1982):104–10.

Johnson, Glen M. "Stephen Crane's 'One Dash—Horses': A Model of 'Realistic' Irony." *Modern Fiction Studies* 23 (1977–78):571–78.

Karlen, Arno. "The Craft of Stephen Crane." *Georgia Review* 28 (Fall 1974):470–97.

Katz, Joseph. Introduction to *The Portable Stephen Crane*. New York: Viking Press, 1969.

Kazin, Alfred. "The Youth: Stephen Crane." In *An American Procession*, 256–74. New York: Knopf, 1984.

Kent, Thomas L. "The Problem of Knowledge in 'The Open Boat' and 'The Blue Hotel.'" *American Literary Realism, 1870–1910*, 14, no. 2 (1981):262–68.

Klotz, Marvin. "Stephen Crane: Tragedian or Comedian: 'The Blue Hotel.'" *University of Kansas City Review* 27 (March 1961):170–74.

Kwait, Joseph J. "Stephen Crane, Literary Reporter: Commonplace Experience and Artistic Transcendence." *Journal of Modern Literature* 8, no. 1 (1980):129–38.

———. "Stephen Crane and Frank Norris: The Magazine and the 'Revolt' in American Literature in the 1890s." *Western Humanities Review* 30 (Autumn 1976):309–22.

Linder, Lyle D. "'The Ideal and the Real' and 'Brer Washington's Consolation': Two Little-Known Stories by Stephen Crane." *American Literary Realism* 11, no. 1 (1978):1–33.

Maclean, Hugh N. "The Two Worlds of 'The Blue Hotel.'" *Modern Fiction Studies* 5 (Autumn 1959):260–70.

Modern Fiction Studies 5 (1959). Special Number on Stephen Crane.

Morace, Robert A. "Games, Play, and Entertainments in Stephen Crane's 'The Monster.'" *Studies in American Fiction* 9, no. 1 (1981):65–81.

Morris, Wright. "Stephen Crane." In *Earthly Delights, Unearthly Adornments: American Writers as Image-Makers*, 51–57. New York: Harper & Row, 1978.

Spofford, William K. "Stephen Crane's 'The Open Boat': Fact or Fiction?" *American Literary Realism* 12 (Autumn 1979): 316–21.

Studies in The Novel 10 (1978). Special Number on Stephen Crane.

Trachtenberg, Alan. "Experiments in Another Country: Stephen Crane's City Sketches." *Southern Review* 10, no. 2 (April 1974):265–86.

Vanouse, Donald. "Women in the Writings of Stephen Crane: Madonna of the Decadence." *Southern Humanities Review* 12 (Spring 1978):141–48.

Vorpahl, Ben Merchant, "Murder by the Minute: Old and New in 'The Bride

Comes to Yellow Sky.'" *Nineteenth-Century American Fiction* 26 (September 1971): 196–218.

Warner, Michael D. "Value, Agency, and Stephen Crane's 'The Monster.'" *Nineteenth-Century Fiction* 40, no. 1 (1985):76–93.

Warshauer, Gerald E. "Bushwhacked by Reality: The Significance of Stephen Crane's Interest in Rural Folklore." *Journal of the Folklore Institute* 19, no. 1 (January–April 1982):1–15.

Weinig, Sister Mary Anthony Weinig. "Homeric Convention in 'The Blue Hotel.'" *Stephen Crane Newsletter* 2 (Spring 1968):6–8.

Wells, H. G. "Stephen Crane from an English Standpoint." *North American Review.* 171 (August 1900):233–42. Reprinted in *Stephen Crane's Career: Perspectives and Evaluations,* edited by Thomas Gullason, 126–33. New York: New York University Press, 1972.

Wertheim, Stanley. "Stephen Crane and The Wrath of Jehova." *Literary Review* 7, no. 4 (Summer 1964):499–508.

Wolford, Chester. "The Eagle and the Crow: High Tragedy and Epic in 'The Blue Hotel.'" *Prairie Schooner* 51 (1977):260–74.

Anthologies of Criticism

Bassan, Maurice, ed. *Stephen Crane: A Collection of Critical Essays.* Englewood Cliffs, N.J.: Prentice-Hall, 1967.

Katz, Joseph, ed. *Stephen Crane in Transition: Centenary Essays.* DeKalb: Northern Illinois University Press, 1972.

Bloom, Harold, ed. *Modern Critical Views: Stephen Crane.* New York and New Haven: Chelsea House Publishers, 1987.

Gullason, Thomas A., ed. *Stephen Crane's Career: Perspectives and Evaluations.* New York: New York University Press, 1972.

Weatherford, Richard M., ed. *Stephen Crane: The Critical Heritage.* London: Routledge & Kegan Paul, 1973.

Collins, Michael J., and Barbara H. Meldrum, eds. *Under The Sun: Myth and Realism in Western American Literature.* Troy, N.Y.: Whitston Press, 1985.

Biographies

Beer, Thomas. *Stephen Crane: A Study in American Letters.* Garden City, N.J.: Garden City Publishing Company, 1927.

Berryman, John. *Stephen Crane.* Cleveland: World Publishing Co., 1950.

Colvert, James B. *Stephen Crane.* New York: Harcourt Brace Jovanovich, 1984.

Linson, Corwin K. *My Stephen Crane.* Syracuse, N.Y.: Syracuse University Press, 1958.

Bibliography

Solomon, Eric. *Stephen Crane in England*. Columbus: Ohio State University Press, 1965.

Stallman, Robert Wooster. *Stephen Crane: A Biography*. Rev. ed. New York: George Braziller, 1973.

Syracuse University Library Associates *Courier* 21, no. 1 (Spring 1986). Special Stephen Crane Number. Largely biographical.

Index

Index

Index

James, Henry, ix, 105, 108
Jameson, Frederic, 25
Joyce, James, *Dubliners*, 61

Kipling, Rudyard, 93, 105, 128

L'Amour, Louis, 28
Lawrence, Frederic M., 3
Leslie, Amy, ix
Levenson, J. C., 44, 49, 113, 133;
  McClure's Magazine, 50
Linson, Corwin Knapp, 83n18

Mencken, H. L., xi, 115
Miller, J. Hillis, xii
Moore, George, 105
Munroe, Lily Brandon, ix, 93

Nagel, James, 15, 113
Naturalism, 19–21, 23, 25, 26, 48,
  62, 80
Nihilism, 26, 35, 43, 48, 80

Parody, 8, 28–30, 50, 52, 63, 64, 68,
  116
Peck, George W., 50
Pope, Alexander, *Rape of the Lock,
  The*, 52
Porter, Katherine Anne, xii

Realism, 13, 21, 23, 62, 102, 116,
  135, 136
Reid, Whitelaw, 140
Reynolds, Paul Revere, 48, 103, 104
Rodgers, Rodney O., 124
Russell, Lillian, 106

Schoberlin, Captain Melvin, xiii
Social reform, 19, 20, 22, 23; drink,
  42
Solomon, Eric, 50
Sorrentino, Paul, xiii, 89
Stallman, R. W., xiii, 82
Stenger, Louis C. Jr., 3
Stevens, Wallace, xiii–xivn5
Stevenson, Robert Louis, 108
Stewart, Cora [Taylor], ix
Surrealism, 118

Tarkington, Booth, 50
Tennyson, Alfred Lord, "Charge of
  the Light Brigade, The," 57, 58
Thoreau, Henry David, 5
Tolstoy, Count Lev Nikolaevich, x,
  100, 102, 107
Townsend, Edward, 106
Tragedy, xii, 30, 33, 34, 44, 49, 116,
  132
Twain, Mark [Samuel Clemens], x,
  105, 113, 133; "Fenimore
  Cooper's Literary Offenses," 8

Walker, Belle, 102
Warner, Charles Dudley, 50
Weinig, Sister Mary Anthony, 33
Welch, J. Herbert, 102
Wells, H. G., ix, 108, 113, 125
Wertheim, Stanley, xiii, 89
West, Rebecca, 113
Williams, Herbert P., 89, 90

Zola, Emile, 21, 107

About the Author

Chester L. Wolford is associate professor of English and business at The Pennsylvania State University–Behrend College. He has published articles on a variety of authors, including Ben Jonson, Nathaniel Hawthorne, and Miguel de Cervantes. A previous book, *The Anger of Stephen Crane: Fiction and the Epic Tradition,* was published by the University of Nebraska Press. His essay on *The Red Badge of Courage* has been reprinted in *Modern Critical Interpretations: The Red Badge of Courage* and *Modern Critical Views: Stephen Crane.* He is writing a business communications text for Harcourt Brace Jovanovich.

About the Editor

General editor Gordon Weaver earned his B.A. in English at the University of Wisconsin-Milwaukee in 1961; his M.A. in English at the University of Illinois, where he studied as a Woodrow Wilson Fellow, in 1962; and his Ph.D. in English and creative writing at the University of Denver in 1970. He is the author of several novels, including *Count a Lonely Cadence, Give Him a Stone, Circling Byzantium*, and most recently *The Eight Corners of the World* (Vermont: Chelsea Green Publishing Company, 1988). Many of his numerous short stories are collected in *The Entombed Man of Thule, Such Waltzing Was Not Easy, Getting Serious, Morality Play*, and *A World Quite Round*. Recognition of his fiction includes the St. Lawrence Award for Fiction (1973), two National Endowment for the Arts Fellowships (1974, 1989), and the O. Henry First Prize (1979). He edited *The American Short Story, 1945–1980: A Critical History*. He is a professor of English at Oklahoma State University and serves as an adjunct member of the faculty of the Vermont College Master of Fine Arts in Writing Program. Married, and the father of three daughters, he lives in Stillwater, Oklahoma.